AMPLIFIERS

NEGAN

AMPLIFIERS

HOW GREAT LEADERS

MAGNIFY THE POWER OF TEAMS,

INCREASE THE IMPACT
OF ORGANIZATIONS,

AND TURN UP THE VOLUME
ON POSITIVE CHANGE

WILEY

Published by John Wiley & Sons, Inc., Hoboken, New Jersey.

Published simultaneously in Canada.

For general information on our other products and services or for technical support, please contact our Customer Care Department within the United States at (800) 762-2974, outside the United States at (317) 572-3993 or fax (317) 572-4002.

Wiley publishes in a variety of print and electronic formats and by print-on-demand. Some material included with standard print versions of this book may not be included in e-books or in print-on-demand. If this book refers to media such as a CD or DVD that is not included in the version you purchased, you may download this material at http://booksupport.wiley.com. For more information about Wiley products, visit www.wiley.com.

Library of Congress Cataloging-in-Publication Data

Names: Finegan, Tom, author.
Title: Amplifiers : how great leaders magnify the power of teams, increase the impact of
  organizations, and turn up the volume on positive change / Tom Finegan.
Description: Hoboken, New Jersey : Wiley, [2021] | Includes index.
Identifiers: LCCN 2021016723 (print) | LCCN 2021016724 (ebook) | ISBN
  9781119794554 (cloth) | ISBN 9781119794578 (adobe pdf) |
  ISBN 9781119794561 (epub)
Subjects: LCSH: Leadership. | Followership.
Classification: LCC HD57.7 .F5555 2021 (print) | LCC HD57.7 (ebook) | DDC
  658.4/092—dc23
LC record available at https://lccn.loc.gov/2021016723
LC ebook record available at https://lccn.loc.gov/2021016724

COVER DESIGN: PAUL MCCARTHY
COVER ART: © GETTY IMAGES | PIXALOT

SKY100284650_072621

This book is dedicated to Bobby Menges (October 21, 1997–September 8, 2017), a true Amplifier throughout his shortened life. He packed more in his nineteen years than most in their lifetimes.

All of the author's proceeds from this book will be donated to the I'm Not Done Yet Foundation, a 501(c)3 in support of adolescent and young adult (AYA) cancer patients and their families.

www.imnotdoneyetfoundation.org

Contents

Introduction

During a family trip to Sweden a few years ago, I came across the historical Vasa. The Swedish warship from the 1600s stands as an enormous symbol of leadership and followership gone awry. Gustav II Adolf was the King of Sweden between 1611 and 1632. He commissioned the construction of four ships to support his war effort, with one being the most powerful warship in the Baltic. The ship was doomed from the design. The hubris of the king and the enormity of the ship were too much for the ship's lead designer, Henrik Hybertsson. Although he was an experienced ship designer, the size and scale were beyond Hybertsson's experience. However, he designed what the king wanted.

Although it was common for warships in the period to be somewhat top heavy, the experts at the shipyard were convinced that there was too much height and weight above the waterline and far too little ballast to support the buoyancy of the ship. Yet construction continued. The workers and their supervisors at the shipyard were not devoid of national pride, nor did they intend to put an unseaworthy vessel into war. They simply did not have the courage to tell the king, their titled executive or boss, that his vision was flawed.

Prior to the maiden voyage, the ship's captain had thirty men run across the deck to cause it to sway to demonstrate to the vice admiral that the ship was unsafe. After three passes, the captain stopped the demonstration for fear of the ship sinking. Yet even with this knowledge, at the final hour prior to the ship's sailing, the captain, the admiral, and the crew chose to squash their concerns and continue on the perilous mission. After sailing only 1,400 yards, the ship sank during its maiden voyage.

Although they were following the directives of the king, this example shows the flaws in both the king's leadership and the ship workers' followership. The king could not accept truth and criticism, and the followers could not deliver the news. Whereas the responsibility lies on both leader and follower to avoid disastrous, or in the case of the Vasa, fatal, consequences, it is hard for followers to bring bad news to a hubristic leader. However, leaders are rarely effective unless they themselves cut their teeth in followership. Good leaders need good followers. And exceptional followers possess a unique blend of leadership and followership characteristics. These exceptional followers are true Amplifiers.

True Amplifiers look like everyday people, but they produce outsized contributions to society. Racial injustices have existed for hundreds of years, but as a result of the killings of George Floyd, Breonna Taylor, and sadly too many more, we are now seeing the seeds of change begin to take root. The hard truth is there is significant work to do, and some have been doing it for years. John Hope Bryant has been sowing the seeds of change for decades with Operation HOPE. His vision is that if he can help people with economic and financial independence, they can prosper and live a more fulfilling life than previous generations. Bryant is a leader for sure. But a closer look will confirm he is just as strong a follower as he is a leader. In fact, I'd argue that his success as a leader is a direct result of his followership. In this book, we will take a closer look at leaders like John Hope Bryant, assess their followership skills, and define the characteristics of a true Amplifier in action.

As someone who has played baseball my whole life, it isn't surprising that one of my favorite books is *Moneyball* by Michael Lewis. Although I was familiar with what Billy Beane was doing with the Oakland Athletics, I did not know of the origins and the nuance underneath the strategy. Beane reinvented traditional thinking on what statistics matter in player recruitment and development. His new take on talent scouting in fact led to a transformative approach for all professional sports. The same philosophy applies to corporations. Organizations need to look at their employees in an entirely different way. For a century, we have evaluated employees on job competencies, management ability, and leadership. These are definitely important, but they miss the true human capital value in an organization. It misses finding the key followers and thus, the true Amplifiers.

Thirty years ago, my cofounders and I started Clarkston Consulting with a simple desire to genuinely serve our clients and create a rewarding environment for our employees, whom we call *stewards*. We called our employees stewards from the start because we want to emphasize the spirit of service we expect of them for our clients and our colleagues. We have worked with a wide variety of global and diverse companies from startup biotechs, upstart consumer brand disruptors, middle market manufacturing companies, and established global consumer products, life sciences, and retail companies. Over the years, we have helped these companies with their strategies and implemented transformation projects, ultimately exceeding $1 billion in cumulative revenue over the years. As a firm, we have seen many executive leaders in action, as well as leadership demonstrated through high-performance teams. We have also seen companies struggle to change and compete in the marketplace. And we have seen how they overcame those challenges. This book reflects our research and observations over the last three decades, dozens of case studies, and our interactions with thousands of professionals in the workplace.

Throughout my consulting career, I have seen countless examples of how some companies can outperform their peers by tapping into the special employees that have Amplifier qualities. On the flip side, we have seen the negative consequences of companies losing their way by following a crash course set by the executives at the top. What separates performance of the top-quartile and bottom-quartile companies oftentimes is the motives of the people at the top. Understanding these motives is critical to understanding ultimate job performance.

We can also turn to areas outside the corporate world to gather insight into good followership and how that leads to Amplifier behavior. Imagine an electorate who can honestly face facts, sort through fact and fiction, and make truly informed and unemotional decisions. Far too often, we replay or echo information we want to believe, think we should believe (for countless reasons), or are afraid to change our old ideals and don't take the time to critically think for ourselves. Today's political stage across the world is very polarized. This is not productive. But compounded with misinformation and delusional thinking throughout the political spectrum, we end up with suboptimal results. We fail to realize that the pursuit of this misinformation and blind support of a politician or political party hollows our intellectual core and renders us as puppets. More critical, independent, challenging, rigorous thinking is needed because we are assaulted with so much information. We need more true Amplifiers who are not afraid to seek a 360-degree view of the truth, speak truth to power, and redirect the polarization to productive means.

Over the years, I've been a student of leadership and followership and their impact on corporate performance. The theme that has emerged from this study is that it takes a special blend of a professional—an Amplifier—to create and wield the power to magnify corporate outcomes. These people possess the unique combination of strong leadership and followership skills. This book is largely aimed at a corporate audience, but it applies to many other social, political, religious, athletic, and philanthropic organizations. For organizations to succeed, they need true Amplifiers. Amplifiers are the people who intuitively know how to simultaneously influence up, lead others, and execute the mission of the firm. Although some people are natural Amplifiers, we have found the ability to magnify corporate outcomes can be enhanced by developing and nurturing Amplifier styles, motives, and traits. Having worked with numerous companies, large and small, I have been able to see their management teams up close and personal. We have helped to create and execute their business strategies. Whether these companies were winners or losers may have depended in part on their product offerings and the markets they serve, but their success is largely based on the strength of their human capital—their people.

Most people believe that in order to be successful, they must be a leader. That is categorically false. Most successful people are followers. But the magic happens when an individual is a highly effective leader and a highly capable follower. This produces the Amplifier. True Amplifiers are the key to success for great companies. They magnify corporate culture, get the most out of teams, increase the impact of organizations, and turn up the volume on positive change within their companies and society.

It has been fun for me to see and work with individuals who were earmarked as "HiPos" or "high-potential employees" and to see how the organizations groomed them in feeder roles and offered them increasing responsibilities. At the time, I knew these individuals were special, but I always attributed that to their leadership capabilities. This was only true in part. The other part, and some might argue the more important part, is their followership ability and functional job competence. The rare breed of great leader and great follower combined produces true Amplifiers. True Amplifiers are the special employees in great companies that actually make them great.

The book is organized into three main sections. In part 1, we introduce the concept of Amplifiers and why they are so important for corporate success. We then take a deeper dive into the differences and mistakes people make by confusing leadership with titled executives or bosses. When analyzing these differences, we explore the difference and common misunderstanding between leadership and management. Then we take a deeper dive into followership and subordinates to better understand the value of followership in corporate success.

Part 2 of the book focuses on finding and developing Amplifiers in your company. We review how "talent scouting" misses the mark in most companies and lay out several strategies to better find and develop potential Amplifiers throughout the company. We thoroughly analyze leadership, followership, and Amplifier styles, motives, and traits in order to create specific development programs to enhance these characteristics throughout the organization. Throughout the section, several examples of Amplifiers who have had successful careers are highlighted along with their secrets and suggestions on what it takes to be an Amplifier.

In part 3 of the book, we explore how Amplifiers magnify the power of teams and increase the impact of corporate performance for its stakeholders. We dig deeper into the Amplifier effect on corporate strategy and how Amplifiers turn up the volume on positive change and corporate racial justice. Several examples highlighting the positive impact of Amplifiers and negative ramifications on corporate outcomes when there is a lack of Amplifiers can be found throughout this section.

Finally, we close the book with how Amplifiers can amplify life beyond work and create a lasting impact on countless people with whom they interact.

Throughout the book, I use my experience and draw from the collective experiences of my colleagues in the firm. Therefore, there are times where I use first-person references, in other cases I use *we*. I also want to respect the emerging thinking regarding gender pronouns and refrain from using *he, his, she,* or *her* and use *they, their,* or *them* as a singular, nongender version of the pronoun.

Leadership + Followership = Amplifiers

True Amplifiers

Leaders, Bosses, Followers, and Subordinates

The key to unlocking organizational success lies in discovering and deploying the Amplifiers in your company. Amplifiers know how to increase the impact for all key stakeholders through the power of example and by bringing out the best in their colleagues who surround them. These Amplifiers have the power to turn up the volume to enable transformation efforts to be successful or to affect the positive change that a company is seeking for long-term and sustainable health.

Leadership and followership are compared to each other as if they are two different sides of the same coin. Common thinking suggests someone is *either* a leader *or* a follower. We don't often see them as two separate dimensions on differing axes. When we juxtapose leaders and bosses on the one axis, and subordinates and followers on the other, we see a different view on effectiveness. Amplifiers exist at the intersection of great leadership and great followership. When deployed effectively throughout the organization, they magnify the power of the teams that they are either assigned to or with whom they interact.

For the purposes of this book, we use the following definitions to frame the discussion. You will notice that our definitions, especially that of leader, differ from the common search definition on

Google, "the person who leads or commands a group, organization, or country."[1]

Our analysis does not focus on job performance skills or proficiency of the individuals. Our work focuses on the leadership and followership attitudes that drive employee engagement and create long-term differentiated and sustainable cultures. We assume that the capabilities of the individual workers are that they are trained, competent, and perform the expected job duties commensurate with their position. We recognize this is not always the case, but that is not in the scope of our analysis.

Leader	*A person who uses their influence, example, or persuasion <u>to cause</u> others to follow them*
Titled Executive/Boss	*A person who is in charge of or commands a group, team, or function*
Follower	*A person who <u>willingly</u> goes along with and accepts direction from a leader*
Subordinate	*A person lower in rank or position who complies with directives of a superior*

In this book, we make an important distinction between leaders and bosses, but not simply by juxtaposing leadership skills with management skills. Instead, we view leaders and bosses (or titled executives) as different ends of the same leadership continuum. They may hold the exact same job title and have the same responsibilities, but they may operate on different ends of the leadership continuum. Similarly, we view followers and subordinates as two ends to the followership continuum. Leaders are usually also bosses, and followers are usually subordinate to their leaders. The distinguishing factors that push them to one end of the continuum or the other are their individual styles, motives, and traits. These dynamics drive how they interact with others to get work done.

Most people think about leadership and followership as two ends of a continuum. However, in Figure 1.1, we show a matrix of

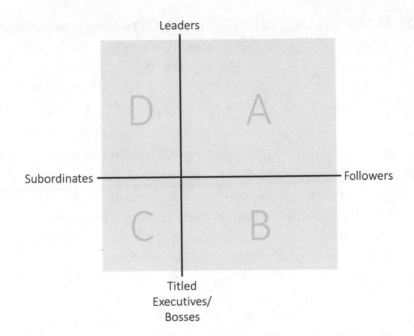

FIGURE 1.1 Leaders, Titled Executives/Bosses, Followers, and Subordinates

leadership and followership behaviors. For the purposes of uncovering and discovering true Amplifiers in an organization, we map leaders and bosses on the same continuum on the vertical axis. We also map followers and subordinates on the same continuum on the horizontal axis. Note the intersection is slightly off-center because most organizations have a higher concentration of leaders and followers.

It is important to note that the actual job function of the person at the top of an organization or function does not differ on the continuum of leaders and bosses. In fact, the activities are the same. We also assume for the purpose of Figure 1.1 that individuals performing their roles are competent; the figure does not evaluate performance but the style in which they carry out their role. What does differ and, in fact, differs significantly, is the style in which they carry out their core job functions. It is the same for followers and subordinates.

Followers and subordinates alike have work to do to complete their daily activities. How they conduct themselves and interact with their colleagues to get that work done is significantly different. The style and the nature of how they approach their work in the context of the broader organization and mission are what sets followers apart from subordinates.

One of the things that is amazing to me is the number of people who share with me their frustration when a colleague who has been promoted to be their boss lacks the requisite leadership skills. These individuals have excelled in their work product, have been exceptional employees, have demonstrated their ability to produce outstanding work, and seem to always reliably get the job done. They possess project planning skills, risk analysis, and the ability to budget and track status. But many times, an individual who possesses these functional subject matter expertise and perhaps even managerial expertise is recognized as a star worker, yet their peers on the team will not follow their lead. When the individual is promoted, the other team members shrug their shoulders in disbelief and commiserate with each other that they will now need to take direction from this newly promoted boss.

Why is it that some people amass followers and others do not? It's easy to spot a leader; just look for their followers. This is very different than looking for a manager and spotting their subordinates. For all the literature on leadership, there is very little that gets after the root cause to know why some people earn followers and some never will. Leaders have found ways to engage and inspire followers that may not exist in mere managers or bosses. Leaders need followers. Yet many leaders don't always understand the reason why their followers follow. Leaders may employ various methods to get work done, two of which are position power and influence. Leaders use these tools at different times for different types of work that needs to be done.

Position power stems from the formal authority vested in the leader simply because of their position in the organization's hierarchy.

Position power enables the leader to force others to take action. It can be extremely effective at getting a lot of work done in a short period of time. Many leaders rely on position power when prompt action needs to occur or when they know they need some quick wins in order to gain broader momentum throughout the organization. But getting work done through position power is not sustainable as a long-term leadership strategy because it generally leads to resentment and disengagement by followers.

Conversely, leaders who rely on influence to get work done by their followers are able to use persuasion to convince the follower to take action. Influence is most effective when the leader has already established a strong relationship with the follower. The follower in turn trusts and respects the leader. This can be motivational for followers. Influence is far more sustainable because influence is the fuel for the engine of followership.

When you are the boss, people think you have followership. What you actually have are people executing orders or following your directions. Tim Hassinger, former CEO of Dow AgroSciences, shared with me one of his secret strategies for checking himself as he progressed throughout his career. "Leaders need to challenge themselves frequently. Honestly ask yourself: do they listen to me because I had a good idea or because I am the boss?" It's critical, especially for new bosses, to sit back and honestly self-assess this question. Everyone who gets promoted has typically received positive affirmation throughout their career. After being promoted to a position that oversees a team, department, business unit, or organization, leaders need to step back and have a regular method for self-appraisal by asking this key question.

Although challenging, the best organizations are able to differentiate between subordinates carrying out the boss's directions and followers who are genuinely inspired by their leader. Most evaluation systems and performance review processes do an excellent job on the measurable elements of job performance. Many have attempted to uncover or discover leadership traits and how they may apply to the individual, which can be fraught with implicit or explicit bias. However, few organizations evaluate or emphasize followership. In order for us to more fully understand leadership, we need to better understand followership. This is important because an Amplifier exists at the intersection of leadership and followership.

Let's look back at Figure 1.1. In quadrant A, we have the special blend of an organization that has leadership and followership. When companies and their corporate culture display behaviors that exist in this quadrant, they produce extraordinary results. The other interesting attribute about quadrant A is that here leaders and followers create legions of leaders and followers throughout the organization. When the flywheel is moving in this quadrant, organizations tend to dominate their markets.

The secret to how great leaders magnify the power of teams, increase the impact of organizations, and turn up the volume on positive change rests in unlocking these operating styles of the cream of the crop of the employee base in companies. The prized intersection of top-performing leaders and the top-performing followers are what we call *Amplifiers*. True Amplifiers are the key group of people in any company who activate the true potential of all stakeholders. Remember, employees can be in any quadrant regardless of their level within the company.

In Figure 1.2, true Amplifiers exist in upper right of quadrant A. These individuals possess the unique combination of leadership and followership skills. They are able to separate the flash leadership behaviors with the lasting leadership behaviors. They stand up and lead up, not just down and across. True Amplifiers have the ability to speak truth to power and influence leaders to change course. Great companies are unceasingly searching and developing Amplifiers throughout the organization regardless of title, tenure, or position.

On a bitterly cold and windy night in the fourth quarter of 2018, I had the opportunity to meet former Massachusetts governor Deval Patrick. My partner and I had spent a long day at Bain Capital's Boston

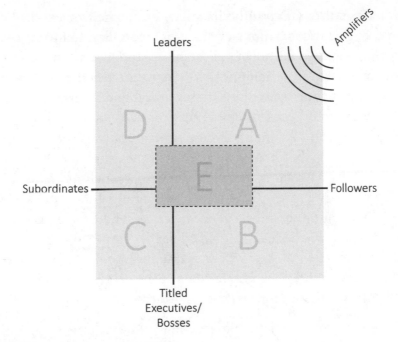

FIGURE 1.2 True Amplifiers

headquarters negotiating the sale of one of our businesses. Patrick had a long list of accomplishments during his eight-year term as governor of Massachusetts. His key priorities were to expand affordable health care, launch initiatives to stimulate clean energy and biotechnology, invest in education, and guide the state through economic crisis to a 25-year high in employment. After he left office, Patrick joined Bain Capital to help launch an impact investing fund. This innovative new fund—Bain Capital Double Impact—is designed to invest in mission-driven companies that target social good, while also generating impressive returns for investors. This chapter in his private work life was an amplification of his belief that private companies can be a force for public good.

I learned through our conversations that what makes Patrick himself a strong leader is that he is an exemplary follower. Over the years, he has been focused on effecting change and is driven by a higher purpose. The combination of competitive spirit and will to succeed coupled with positive examples from some remarkable leaders he has served have created the true Amplifier qualities that he so effectively embodies. One of the nicest things that his team said about him when he left the justice department was that when it was time to sign off on a case from the civil rights department, the section leader would present, and Patrick would go around the table and ask everyone for input. Even if a paralegal was there, he'd ask them what ideas they had. It wasn't something they were accustomed to. But he was constantly learning and got so much more out of the team by engaging each of them that he magnified their impact. Patrick had the humility to be a good leader, to subordinate his ego and pull ideas out of the team. He railed at the "imperial CEO," whose feet never touched the ground, everything was looked after for them, and they lost sight of the implications of the decisions and impact to stakeholders because they were shielded from reality.

Quadrant B is an interesting quadrant insofar as it is composed of strong followers who lack leadership skills. For teams that report to executives in Quadrant B, true Amplifiers are critically important. The followers need to shore up the leadership gaps of their bosses in order to lead the team to achieve its mission and purpose. Organizations can be incredibly successful, even lack the institutional leadership, if they have followership en masse. I've seen firsthand over the years some very successful companies with great brands or products that have had marginal leaders at the top but have had outstanding key lieutenant followers in executive positions. These organizations, or functions within an organization, outlive the titled executive or boss. Followers and true Amplifiers can coexist with bosses or non-leaders in a particular function, but they are motivated and motivate others for a variety of reasons. In some cases, it's the higher purpose of the company. In other cases, it may be their career aspirations. But over time, they will need to have superiors who are higher on the leadership scale or they will self-select to another area within the company or outside the company altogether.

Quadrant C is much more problematic. However, a number of companies exist with a large employee population in quadrant C.

Quadrant C is where incremental progress occurs. Many companies can still be effective in the short run. This quadrant is full of low-profile companies operating at a baseline level of performance. In some cases, they operate in product or service sectors that are fully mature. These companies are rich acquisition targets due to their lack of revenue growth, operating performance, and steady cash flows. Alternatively, companies that exist in this quadrant were once high-flyers and have grown significantly but have evolved into a style of incremental management. They are too big to be acquired or too far beyond the ability to affect positive change. They have become large zombie companies.

Quadrant D is the most precarious. In this quadrant, there is strong leadership, potentially flash leadership in an organization filled with individuals who will carry out the tasks. Think of the individuals at Tyco in the procurement or accounts payable department who were responsible for buying and paying the bill for CEO Dennis Kozlowski's gold toilet seat or the toga party for his wife's birthday. In this example, there is a strong cultlike personality at the top job of the company. He had enough leadership, at least temporarily, to influence subordinates to engage in his outrageous behavior.

Another example is the GE travel team who allowed Jeffrey Immelt to have a backup jet available on each of his travel visits so that he would not be delayed. The enablement of these cultlike celebrity CEOs is the antithesis of good followership. Quadrant D is littered with bankrupt companies or companies that have fallen from grace. It is in this quadrant where more shareholder, employee, and societal damage occurs than anywhere else. Other traps in this quadrant consist of serial acquisitions with marginal payoffs. With this strategy, CEOs are often heralded in the media as rock stars because of the growth of the companies they have been tasked to manage. But debt and goodwill swells resulting in a magnified risk in the balance sheet. In a low-interest-rate environment, the strategy can be pursued for some time. Inevitably though, companies that pursue this strategy run out of runway and they crash and burn. One disastrous example was the strategic pursuit of Valeant Pharmaceuticals from 2008 to 2016 under the direction of CEO Michael Pearson. His rampant buying spree was a terrible long-term strategy, although his methods artificially propped up the stock price for a short and unsustainable period of time.

Obviously, it's not as simple as individuals existing in a particular quadrant for all the roles they play within the company. Most of what we do needs to interoperate among the many hats we wear when executing our jobs. For example, an executive vice president in an organization clearly needs to have strong leadership skills *and* strong followership skills. They may be responsible for leading geographic regions, strategic business units, or major operational functions. Despite these clear responsibilities, they are also a subordinate follower to their leaders. This dynamic highlights how closely aligned leadership and followership are and, when combined, can produce extraordinary results.

Simply because an individual or company exists in a particular quadrant does not mean they will stay there indefinitely. We've seen companies drift or change over time. It is usually the case when there is a major change in strategic direction, market conditions, shareholder activism, or CEO succession. This leads us to dig deeper to understand what the characteristics are for individuals in each of the quadrants. It also leads us to understand leading indicators that may demonstrate movement between the quadrants.

2

Leaders Versus Titled Executives

Leadership Differs from Management

Leadership and management are not the same. Amazingly, people often get this wrong. Bosses are frequently confused with leaders, and subordinates are confused with followers. That said, a boss may very well be a leader, but it is not a foregone conclusion. Just because a boss has the title or power in the relationship, doesn't mean that boss is a leader. We have all seen these bosses in action—the titled executive or manager who oversees a large team but has no followers. Some employees do as they are instructed by the boss, but not because they are being led or because those employees are drawn to follow, but rather because they fear the boss's reprisals. This is not leadership.

Sometimes we see this demonstrated in nonbusiness settings, such as politics. All too frequently, we find ourselves governed by a politician who, although they were voted into office, they are not an actual leader. These individuals may not even have the credentials to be qualified for the role. Although they certainly have the position, they do not garner a broad following.

My favorite book on explaining the differences between leadership and management is *A Force for Change* by John Kotter. We confuse leadership with people in managerial functions. Kotter lays out the stark differences between mobilizing groups of people in a common direction (leadership) and organizing a group of people to accomplish a task or run a function (management). Kotter makes a special point to parse leadership from the commonly misused title of someone who sits atop a business function or organization, what we call in this book, a *titled executive*.

Kotter rightly argues that simply by virtue of holding a position at the top of a team, department, or an entire organization doesn't imply that the person is actually providing leadership. Despite the book having been written in 1990, we continue to imbue the elements of leadership unwittingly onto these managers and titled executives.

What is amazing, though, is when these teams or departments produce extraordinary results despite the lack of leadership at the top. How is it that teams can function despite this lack of leadership at the top? In some cases, it's momentum from a previous manager. In other cases, the product carries itself. But more commonly, success is driven by followership in action. Professionals who are not in the top spot are able to step up to fill the leadership void by wielding influence among their peers.

What motivates people to fill the leadership gap left by their managers? Some employees are motivated by their own career aspirations, seeing the void as an opportunity to demonstrate their capabilities. Others are motivated by serving the customer out of a need to simply do the right thing. These employees are driven by the greater purpose their organization is pursuing.

Titled managers or executives have power. Simply by nature of their title or position, these bosses can get others to do their work. Confusing this with leadership can lead to disastrous results. Some companies mistakenly have managers run leadership development training sessions. Such training sessions likely merge the concepts of leadership and management, but these two disciplines require very different skills. Companies can and should train separately for good management and for good leadership. Far too often, companies conflate the two and they wonder why the results are suboptimal.

Leaders do not need to be good managers, but depending on how high up in the organization the position, good management requires leadership. We have seen many good leaders who cannot manage well. If these good leaders are self-actualized, they recognize that they need to have good followers who are also good managers. They can delegate the management skill far more effectively than a follower can fill a leadership void.

Management Matters

There is an abundance of research on the science of management, and much has been written about how to manage more effectively. The "modern" father of management discipline is Peter Drucker in his 1973 book, *Management*. A significant amount of derivative work has been written based on his principles. Many of the current-day management philosophies are driven by his concepts. Even as these management practices have evolved over the past decades since Drucker wrote his material, little work has been done to discover traits that make great workers great.

Unlike theories on management, which focus on the "elite few," very little has been written on individual contributors. Yet these individuals—those who are being managed—make up the majority of employees at many companies and are largely responsible for carrying out the organization's strategic goals. Understanding workers—whether they are subordinates or followers—is a worthwhile study for any leader or manager. Flipping the management theory coin and taking a closer look at employees who are being managed reveals greater insight into how to achieve higher performance from those teams.

Delving into the prevailing wisdom on management highlights several key gaps. We are increasingly operating in a world with a greater number of remote or virtual workers, especially because we've experienced a forced work-from-home environment during the global COVID-19 pandemic in 2020 and 2021. Managing these remote workers requires a different set of tools. Managers cannot manage by walking around, pulling subordinates in for quick conversations in real time, or interacting easily with workers in an informal manner. Culture trumps strategy, and building a strong culture with remote workers is difficult. All these factors and others necessitate the use of differing methods and tools to connect with workers. The effectiveness of these tools remains questionable as the modern workforce grapples with how best to deploy them.

Another change in how knowledge workers get work done is the agile method of running projects and accomplishing work. This style democratizes the nature of work, placing more emphasis on the workers responsible for getting the work done than on the managers overseeing the teams. The following summarizes a few key characteristics of good workers.

Subject Matter Aspects
- Subject matter expertise or competency
- Accreditation and special training
- Company and industry knowledge

Technical Aspects
- Project planning and oversight
- Team construction and oversight
- Problem deconstruction and solving
- Risk management and contingency planning

Nontechnical and People Aspects
- Communication
- Performance management
- Professional development

Administrative Aspects
- Risk and issue resolution and management
- Budgeting and forecasting
- Goal setting and tracking
- Compliance

Traditional Leadership

"If you think you are a leader and you are out there and turn around and there's nobody behind you, you're not a leader, just a guy out there taking a walk."

—John Hope Bryant

There is so much confusion regarding what leadership is and what it is not. There is an abundance of books and articles written about leadership. Many universities have courses devoted to studying leadership. But far too often we miss the point. Simply because someone occupies a chair does not make them a leader. Additionally, leaders with charisma or popularity can seduce employees by their style. When we follow these individuals, we often find ourselves in regrettable positions.

What's more, we often feel that leadership is good when that is not necessarily the case. I was in a bookstore several years ago browsing business books and noticed the title of the book, *Bad Leadership* written by Barbara Kellerman. The main premise of the book is that there have been some great leaders, who have inspired countless followers, into horrible outcomes. This is true on the world stage, as shown by Adolph Hitler, as well as in the business world, as shown by Dennis Kozlowski at Tyco or Jeffrey Skilling at Enron. I used to think of these individuals as horrible leaders. However, when evaluating them in the context of their ability to persuade others to follow, they were actually great leaders with bad motives or bad styles that led to horrible outcomes. Although we may not agree with the direction a leader is taking, it is dangerous to deny that individual is a leader. They, in fact, check many of the leadership boxes, display numerous leadership traits, and ultimately are successful as measured by the number of followers they amass.

Let's take a fresh look at leadership. Leadership is tricky. The ways in which some leaders successfully inspire followers could be disastrous approaches for others. We also need to look at leadership within the context of time. The leadership examples Kellerman uses in her book clearly show leadership capabilities, but are they lasting? What is the shelf life of leadership? History reveals truly great leaders that produced great outcomes. History also reveals the flash-in-the-pan leadership, the kind of leadership that sprouts up to fill some void or deficiency in an organization but does not last. We don't have the benefit of hindsight in the moment. And unfortunately, many people don't fully exercise their critical thinking when they're in the moment. These followers may be overcome by emotion, false information, echo chambers, delusion, greed, power, or other self-serving motives.

One of my favorite debates is whether a trait such as leadership or entrepreneurialism is born or learned behavior. It's hard to watch toddlers, barely able to walk, in a playground and not see leaders and followers in action. There is already something psychologically at play with these children causing one to lead and another to follow. Could it have been the development for the first twelve months or is it DNA? It is likely a bit of both. There is an instinct, environment, and development aspect for leadership.

Leaders ascend to their role in a variety of ways. They may inherit the role, as in the case of King Gustav Adolf (see the introduction), or they may be appointed, elected, or promoted based on the Peter principle, when people tend to rise only to their level of competence. Over the years in my consulting assignments, I've been able to work with some of the world's most respected global companies. I'm amazed that no one is alarmed at how imperfect performance management processes and talent outcomes are not a higher priority to correct. The investment in talent development pays dividends for all involved. When this is compounded over decades, organizations may end up with poorly equipped executives to lead the company. The biggest failure in these performance management processes is that they fail to recognize the role exemplary followers play in their manager's success. We've seen credit given to, and readily accepted by, a mid-level manager or executive when they were largely a bystander of the success. Many times, it is the Amplifiers who in fact brought the initiative to a successful conclusion. Organizations that can effectively parse the elements of success among the entirety of the team in an unbiased way generally do a better job of promoting the right people.

Leadership in sports is another fascinating topic. Years ago, Chuck Knoll, the famed head coach of the Pittsburg Steelers, spoke to our company about teamwork. What struck me was that the Steelers organization was filled with professional athletes, all heralded as leaders as they progressed to the highest levels of football. The Steelers won four Super Bowl titles under the Hall of Fame quarterback, Terry Bradshaw. Yet Knoll said if he had eleven Bradshaws on the field at the same time, he would not have won a single game. Knoll was making two critical points about skill and leadership. Each of the eleven players on the field needed the skills to play their position and play it well. Equally important was that the eleven players on the field needed to play the play that was called by the quarterback in the huddle or the audible prior to the snap.

The interchange between leaders and followers makes the difference between good organizations or teams and great ones. Feedback received by Bradshaw enabled him to be better at his position, call better plays, and better position the team to win on the field leading to championships. If he wasn't on his game, his teammates let him know. They challenged him and their fellow teammates alike. This give-and-take of feedback created a championship team. The entire team had a common goal, and they worked together to continue to raise the bar of their performance.

The most effective leaders are driven by something greater than themselves. They intuitively know how to create an environment where their followers are willing to go the extra mile to support them and, many times, adopt a selfless leadership style. Think back over your career and note where you have been motivated to work for a boss who cared more about themselves than they did for others. We aren't typically motivated to follow these individuals.

In their book, *The Trusted Advisor*, David Maister, Charlie Green, and Robert Galford create the trust equation, which simply states that trustworthiness = (credibility + reliability + intimacy) / self-interest. Increasing self-interest destroys results-oriented traits such as credibility and reliability. In other words, if the individual is self-interested, it doesn't matter how good they are—there is always an element of mistrust that will exist. This mistrust erodes the leader's effectiveness.

Helena Foulkes is a remarkable business leader and true Amplifier. After getting her MBA at Harvard, she joined CVS, where she had a very impressive career ultimately ascending to executive vice president of CVS Health and president of CVS Pharmacy. After leaving a successful career at CVS, she took the position of CEO and a board member of Hudson's Bay Company.

Great leaders like Foulkes understand the power of connecting with people and engaging their ideas and building trust. She would do this in various "skip-level" meetings or when she was interacting in the stores or directly with consumers. One of the followership skills she emphasized was the muscle of "returning authority," which occurs when the leader delegates certain decisions on strategic approaches that need to be made throughout the organization. The important element of returning authority is that you don't take it back. The teams need to understand the boundaries and general alignment of the top-level strategy or approach, but they are empowered to carry out the activities necessary to bring that element of the strategy or plan to fruition. For new leaders, this is often one of their biggest challenges. Most leaders grew up doing the activities themselves and it's hard to watch teams that report to them work through some of the same issues or do things slightly differently than they would have. Being a good leader is about empowering these teams to learn during the journey while ensuring that the expected outcomes are in fact achieved. The higher up the organization leaders ascend, the more critical it is for those leaders to lead effectively by returning authority and fostering that mutual trust.

The Charisma Trap ━━━━━━━━━━━━━━━━━━━━━━━━━

Charisma is a red herring in leadership. *Merriam-Webster* defines charisma as, "i) a personal magic of leadership arousing special popular loyalty or enthusiasm for a public figure (such as a political leader), or ii) a special magnetic charm or appeal."[1] These are not essential elements of leadership. Helpful, yes. Essential, no. Effective leadership does require influencing others to follow. But that influence can come through a variety of ways.

The antonym of *charisma* is *repulsive*. In 2020, we lived during a time when we had a political leader whose style simultaneously created an equally large following and a large repulsiveness (detractors). True leadership has to be more comprehensive and capture a greater share of potential followers. It is unrealistic to think that the leader will never have detractors. And the best leaders use these detractors to actually hone their leadership skills.

Another way to look at charisma in leadership is the old saying, "it's all sizzle and no steak." Individuals who ascend the organizational hierarchy through personality and charisma, but lack competence become ineffective. Because they lack the content or experience to effectively lead, their charisma carries them only so far. Charismatic individuals can stand on stage and engage their audience whether they are speaking truth or not. They tap into what the audience wants to hear and feed off their insecurities or wishful thinking. Perpetuating the delusional thinking or party line becomes the core tool in the arsenal.

Unfortunately, we see too many individuals promoted to leadership positions who lack the necessary leadership skills. Worse, some are elected to high office and lack the leadership skills to capture followers in a comprehensive way. True leaders are able to capture followers, despite differences of opinion or approaches.

In his book, *Good to Great*, Jim Collins identified his "Level 5" leader as having a paradoxical blend of personal humility and professional will. Charisma and humility can and do coexist for many leaders. Being humble does not mean being a doormat. It simply means lacking the arrogance in belief that they have all the answers and can do no wrong. Individuals who ascend organizations with increasing responsibility typically have received positive feedback and have likely had limited negative criticism. This continuous positive feedback loop can have a detrimental impact on the executive's humility. When surrounded by "yes" people, these leaders run the risk of not developing the kind of humility needed for true leadership as Collins describes.

Some of the best leaders are not well-known charismatic individuals. Take Larry Culp, the first externally hired CEO at General Electric (GE) in decades. Prior to leading GE, Culp was the CEO of Danaher Corporation, having taken the helm at about the same time Jeffrey Immelt took over as CEO of GE from Jack Welch. Whereas the stock of GE *fell* significantly by more than 30 percent under Immelt, Danaher's stock price rose nearly 500 percent under Culp for the same time period.[2] Yet we constantly saw Immelt on magazine covers, high-profile political appointments on committees, major conference speaking events, and the like. Culp had a significantly lower profile and was not heralded as a celebrity CEO. He was simply more effective and possessed a significantly more down-to-earth style. To be sure, Culp is in the early innings of turning around GE and time will tell if he will be effective on that transformation journey. In the two-and-a-half years on the job GE's stock is up a modest 1 percent, trailing the broader averages.

Another Level 5 leader Amplifier is Dan Caulkins, the president and CEO of Benjamin Moore & Co. He started at the company nearly 30 years ago as a sales correspondent, a job that no longer exists. Shortly after Caulkins was promoted onto the executive team, there was a change at the CEO level. All his peers in the executive suite applied for the CEO job, except Caulkins. He got a call from the HR leader and Warren Buffett asking him why he didn't apply. He explained that given where the organization was at the time and what was needed to transform the culture and operational performance, he did not feel he possessed the skills necessary to be successful in the role. The organization had gone through significant turmoil over the previous six or seven years and he felt like they needed a leader who could calm the waters and take the craziness out of the day-to-day. He emphasized that he did think he could be the CEO of the company someday, but he personally didn't feel like that time was now. He recognized that if it had been him at the time, it would have been about him and his agenda. Bringing in someone else provided the opportunity for a fresh and unbiased view that was not threatening. This new leader and Caulkins worked together to shore up the gaps he had in order to be successful in the CEO position he now holds.

Caulkins is self-actualized. He has a realistic and balanced view regarding what he is good at and where he relies on his team's strengths to round out the capabilities at the top. He recognizes that all executives, like all humans, have an ego. And that the positive accolades that come with career progression are fuel for the ego. He is quick to recognize that effective leaders need to check their ego at the door and be comfortable admitting when they don't know something and delegating to the experts on their team. His perspective is that the role of the leader is to help with resource allocation, answer the questions of what we are going to do, why are we going to do it, and how can we do it. He has seen too many leaders who are afraid to admit their weaknesses. Paradoxically, it's the leaders who admit and embrace their weaknesses and mistakes that create more followers than those who deny or cover them up.

There is a bell curve that highlights the relationship of the charismatic leader and the perils of having too much. We call it the *charisma trap*. There is a baseline level of charisma necessary for leaders to lead any organization, but correspondingly too much charisma may lead to negative results. In Figure 2.1, we look at leadership effectiveness and level of charisma.

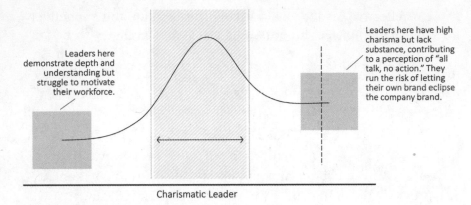

Leaders here demonstrate depth and understanding but struggle to motivate their workforce.

Leaders here have high charisma but lack substance, contributing to a perception of "all talk, no action." They run the risk of letting their own brand eclipse the company brand.

Charismatic Leader

FIGURE 2.1   Charismatic Leader Trap

The good news for the introverted leaders is that charisma can be taught. The bad news, when charisma goes too far, the leader may display a tendency toward narcissistic behavior. Unlike leadership development to flex and develop charisma, narcissism is difficult, if not impossible, to mute. There is a high correlation to overly charismatic personalities—those who thrive on self-aggrandizement- and narcissism. It is important to note that leaders bent on self-interest still emerge in business, though most lead to their own self-serving causes—such as Jeffrey Skilling from Enron or Dennis Kozlowski from Tyco, as well as some prominent political leaders. Although they certainly have followers, these individuals are fooled into supporting this narcissistic leader to serve the leader's self-seeking causes. For these highly charismatic celebrity CEOs, the risk is that they are pursuing their own gratification and pulling followers along for the ride. Once the leader develops a narcissistic reputation, there is little hope to regain trust in the organization. In the *Trusted Advisor*, Maister, Green, and Galford describe how self-orientation erodes trust.

True Amplifiers are essential when the leader lacks charisma and especially helpful when the leader displays tendencies of narcissism. Effective organizations need visionary motivation, but when the leader lacks this critical skill, true Amplifiers can effectively fill this gap. An effective leader would recognize this gap and proactively lean on a key follower to amplify the vision and strategy.

On the other extreme, when the leader is in the zone of potential narcissism, the Amplifier becomes even more critical. The narcissistic leader finds it difficult to separate their personal brand from the corporate brand. They believe that they are the reason for any successes the company may have. They invest in their personal brand and self-promotion at similar levels to the corporate brand. To offset this style, the true Amplifier can become a necessary sounding board to the organization to help build or enhance trust in leadership by redirecting feelings of resentment. Organizations need to understand that the leaders have their back, and the Amplifier can do this when the leader is unable.

Titled Executives and Bosses

Virtually all organizations have bosses and titled executives. In an ideal world, the people who fill those positions are also leaders. Employees carry out the wishes of these individuals either because of their position power or their influence. Most humans don't want to be told what to do. They want to be led or inspired to take the next right action. It's this basic human instinct that effective leaders need to understand.

Most companies have a formal organizational chart with predefined job titles and promotion criteria. They evaluate employees across a broad spectrum of competencies. However, many capitulate and promote employees because they have been in a particular position for such a long period, or they put pressure on their managers so that they will look elsewhere if they don't get the promotion. Publicly, companies deny they promote based on these real factors, but privately they admit that is what happens. We engage with some of the best and most respected firms, yet we see this practice in action far too frequently. The Peter principle is alive and well. There is a gap between the espoused courage to make disciplined promotion decisions and the capitulation to employee pressure. Each time a company compromises a promotion decision or a crucial performance management discussion, they erode a bit of competitive advantage or slightly increase the odds that their next transformation effort will fail. The compounding effect of these suboptimal decisions is astounding.

Titled executives or bosses lack some or most of the leadership traits necessary to be an effective leader. Therefore, they need different tools to get their subordinates to act. The primary tool they turn to is fear. Fear is an easy human emotion to tap into. Most people are afraid of not achieving something they don't have or losing something they do have. In the business context, this translates to fear of not being promoted to the next level, with the additional recognition and monetary rewards associated with the move. At the extreme, it can mean the fear of losing a job. Another tool these bosses use is a high degree of control, as they rule with an iron fist. These bosses are referred to as micromanagers. They feel the need to be involved in every decision, review every piece of work before it goes out, and other non-empowering and nonproductive behaviors that waste time and resources.

The fascinating reality of titled executives is that in a quiet moment by themselves, they often recognize their lack of leadership. They have a high ego with an inferiority complex. The style becomes one of lashing out to squash an uprising among dissenting voices and reassignment of star performers who might make them look bad. They surround themselves with "yes" people to reinforce their own ideas and positions. To be fair, many executives do not intentionally choose this path. But somehow, their ego and high need for power drive them into this operating style.

Tim Hassinger, introduced in chapter 1, spent three decades with increasing levels of responsibility and leadership within the same company, ultimately becoming the CEO of a major division. This led him to being recruited and accepting the CEO position of a publicly traded company. Joining a new company after such a long tenure at the previous employer provided new opportunities for learning and growth. He no longer knew the large numbers of employees who worked for him, nor had deep institutional knowledge of the culture and how change would need to occur. He knew he needed to learn these dynamics and learn quickly. Likewise, the organization itself needed to come to terms with the fact that a new outside CEO had been brought in to effect change and set a new direction for the company.

In this situation, Hassinger was immediately placed in a position where the answer to the question "are people following me because of my role or my influence?" was clear. For new leaders appointed from the outside, the initial set of followers are following because of position power. The challenge then becomes how to quickly gain influence throughout the organization and how to determine the composition of followers on staff. It's natural in a leadership transition that many alienated follower holdovers will leave. Many pragmatist followers will also leave with a leadership change at the top, especially one where stated change is necessary, which undermines the very safety that pragmatist followers require. The exemplary followers under the previous leadership likely have loyalty to each other, the organization, or the mission. However, these exemplary followers will quickly size up the new leader to determine whether or not they will follow them.

When new CEOs are appointed or promoted, one of the first activities they do is to replace key team members. Jim Collins emphasizes the necessity for great companies to have "the right people on the bus."[3] How then do companies find themselves in this position where the new CEO needs to make these replacements? Great companies are constantly adjusting the team at the top to have the best possible executive leadership—or in management teams throughout the company for that matter. But, far more commonly, teams evolve and settle into their operating ruts, and before you know it, there are weak links in the chain.

Cross-functional teams and matrixed organizational structures create more of a challenge for the titled executive. In this construct, their straight-line chain of control is pierced by the matrix. In situations when the executive lacks leadership experience, infighting and turf wars emerge. It is amazing to see how many companies have these unnecessary internal skirmishes when the real adversary is a competitor or product substitute.

Instead, the most successful organizations also create dynamic, or in some cases permanent, cross-functional teams. Assembling these cross-functional teams is as important as assembling a proper organizational chart. One of the traps leaders have is that they pick the same people for high-profile teams. This is dangerous for many reasons. Selection bias is an issue for most companies, and many are trying to address this bias with varying degrees of success. Executives and managers within companies tend to select people who are like them to fill positions on teams. This perpetuates narrow thinking and prevents the true diversity of thought and ideas that is necessary for the best decision-making to occur.

Some professionals are driven entirely by status. Status can be achieved in many different ways. Status can be achieved by the position you occupy in the organizational chart as well as how many teams you've been chosen to participate in. There is a real risk in assigning the same people to too many teams, letting teams become too large and unwieldy or not sunsetting teams when their stated purpose has been accomplished. The best leaders and executives shared a common theme with me in how they peer into critical team composition and assignments to ensure that each team member actively participates and quickly jettison team members who seem to be observers only. They look at a network analysis of the core strategic teams in the company. This conscious effort to analyze and remove people from teams is as essential as ensuring that the teams themselves are composed of key decision-makers and influencers to be successful. Finally, although it's impossible to limit the size of certain teams, smaller teams with a clear objective seem to fare better in any organization.

Leadership Lessons: The 20-60-20 Rule

Early in my tenure as CEO of our firm, I was agonizing over another seemingly big decision that I needed to make that I knew was not going to be popular with everyone. I say seemingly because in hindsight I can't recall most of the decisions I agonized over. But I would stew over them desperately wanting complete approval from the hundreds of consultants who worked for us. After sufficient discussion and review of our options, the time would come when we made the decision, and I would communicate the decision to the broader company. Feedback would come back to us and even in situations where I felt the decision was entirely negative yet necessary, I would get emails or texts from people letting me know they appreciated the decision and were fully supportive of the direction. The more this occurred the more I realized that in most big controversial decisions, people fall into the "20-60-20 rule". Twenty percent of the people think the decision is genius, 20 percent of the people think the decision is a disaster and wonder how we ever got to the position we're in, and 60 percent of the people trust that it's probably best and move on. This realization lets us sit back and weigh the decisions we're making and filter them through the 20-60-20 rule so that we could ask ourselves, "Will this decision or direction skew the distribution?" As a leader it's impossible, and in fact not wise, to never piss people off. As is frequently referenced by Colin Powell, sometimes it's necessary to piss people off. Once I no longer felt the need to have everyone's approval for every decision we made, it liberated me to make decisions much more effectively.

3

Followers Versus Subordinates

What really makes managers effective is a good team of employ-ees. Some of these employees are subordinates, and many are followers. There are important distinctions between subordinates and followers. Effective managers can get subordinates to deliver output at a high level of productivity. However, followers not only have the capacity to produce high-quality work but also to amplify the manager's effectiveness. Great managers recognize that excep-tional followers have the ability to transform how the organization can deliver superior results. Being able to identify followers from a sea of subordinates is important to drive that success.

Subordinates

Anyone who has been responsible for managing staff members understands the difference between an employee who is strictly a subordinate and one who is a follower. In some cases, subordinates are actually easier to manage. Because they tend not to employ criti-cal independent thinking skills for their given assignment, they will simply carry out the orders or directions you give them. However, they may require more interaction because they are less capable of resolving issues or any nonconforming item that comes up in their workflow, process, or assembly.

Good subordinates do as they are told, typically no more and no less. Employees with this operating style are generally easy to predict and can produce reliable and repeatable output in their tasks or position. However, because they lack critical independent thinking skills, they are susceptible to leaders with bad motives or ill-conceived strategies. Any company with a large percentage of subordinates versus followers runs the risk of pursuing a failed course and underachieving their potential.

Subordinates are motivated to work because they have to; it's a necessary evil. They have mixed, if any, career aspirations. Their work is a job, not a vocation. However, being a subordinate in and of itself is not a bad thing. Most companies, including great companies, have a large number of subordinates among their workforces. Great companies are able to channel the energy of these hard-working and dutiful employees toward the ultimate mission and destination of the company strategy. Furthermore, they are able to spot subordinates with followership potential and raise them up along the followership continuum in order to tap their skills and unleash greater career potential for them as professionals.

Many subordinates are not qualified to become managers, and in fact, many do not aspire to manage others. Some subordinates are seasonal, transient, or in entry-level positions that are hired for a particular individual contributor role where management responsibilities do not make sense. That said, subordinates are core team members and are essential for the company's success.

The characteristics of subordinates are quite different than those of followers:

- **Competency.** Many subordinates are very capable at their core job responsibilities. They typically don't need heavy supervision, have learned their jobs well, and are able to effectively get their work done. They can track down issues, interact with business partners and colleagues, and generally resolve barriers to getting the job done. Managers seldom have to worry about them getting off task or if their work product will be done accurately and on time.

- **Work ethic.** Many subordinates have a proven work ethic. When faced with milestone dates, surge capacity, or the daily grind of the workload, they have the inner drive to persist and get the job done. Managers can rely on these workers to work on tasks until the job is complete.
- **Reliability and consistency.** One of the great assets of subordinates is that they are reliable. As the business environment, workload, or the work itself changes, subordinates are steadfast and get the work done. They are consistent. Managers can depend on these workers in good times and bad to carry out the mission of the group.
- **Ownership.** Subordinates believe the job you task them with is theirs. They do not need to be reminded to complete their tasks or to complete their work with the utmost care because they take pride and ownership of their work.

As strong as these characteristics are and the value they bring to managers, subordinates don't possess the leadership or followership traits necessary to fill a leadership void. They can be counted on to get their job done and done well, but their primary focus will be on their individual responsibilities. They are unlikely to ascend to higher leadership or management roles because they are unable to engage a broader group to amplify output. They are perfectly content being position players and sometimes can be in their roles for long periods of time. Yet organizations cannot succeed without them. They are a critical part of the organization's success. Conversely, some subordinates possess the requisite skills, albeit in an immature state, and simply need to be developed, like raw clay, so they can become effective followers.

Followership Explained

Far too often, we hear parents ask their children the familiar question and then supply the subsequent statement, "If your friend tells you to jump off a bridge, would you do it? Be a leader, not a follower."

Ironically, what they actually mean is to be a good follower. Don't blindly follow but think independently and take the *right* action. In fact, influence others not to jump as well. But followers are not heralded in society in the same way leaders are. Why is that? We are obsessed with leaders, but we don't spend much time with followers. Followers make the world function.

The Lone Nut

Several years ago, I was introduced to a video clip that quickly became a favorite and one that we use in our leadership development curriculum. The YouTube video of the "lone nut" illustrates the value of followership. The lone nut is a young man at an outdoor concert venue with a modest smattering of people. He starts to dance to the music as an individual in an open section of the field. At first, he is the lone nut dancing among a sea of oglers. Then, one person musters up the courage to join this lone dancer. This first follower makes two. The two dance joyfully until a third individual hesitatingly joins them. Once there are three dancing, others join the group in twos and threes. Some that were at first scoffing at the lone nut look to their friends sitting next to them, shrug their shoulders, and join in. Not only was it now safe for followers to join in but also they might be outcasts if they did not.

This example is not a perfect business example because it takes place at a festival. The individuals did not need to follow to accomplish a transformation effort or fulfill the mission of any organization. They were simply out to have some fun. None risked their career, nor did they have to worry about getting their other work done. But the example does highlight some key elements of leadership and followership.

First, let's look at the lone nut. The lone nut was an individual with an idea; in this case, an idea that there should be dancing at the festival. He demonstrated courage and he took action. He was not a particularly good dancer but his conviction that there ought to be dancing at the festival and that he would lead by example gave him the gumption to take charge. Have you ever found yourself taking a stance that has not yet been expressed? If so, you are playing the role of the lone nut.

Now the first follower is an important distinction. The first follower has that unique blend of leadership and followership characteristics. The first follower is a true Amplifier. Had the first follower never followed the lone nut, the lone nut never would have become a leader. He just remains the lone nut. The first follower needs courage. The first follower does not know if the rest of the crowd will think dancing in an open field is a good idea. The first follower also must display a similar level of courage and action. It is now much safer for the second follower to participate, yet there is still some risk of being ostracized. The lone nut and the first follower have taken some risk out of the equation for the others.

The second follower may be following for a variety of reasons. It might be that they truly respect the lone nut or first follower and will always follow them. It could be that they are bored and open for a new challenge. As the three are dancing in the field and other followers start to join, you can see that the idea is beginning to take hold and that it is now entirely safe for others to join in. As people join the group in twos and threes, more and more people join until there is now a large crowd dancing in the field. What's fascinating to me is that there was no big change management plan necessary to motivate this large crowd to get off their picnic blankets and into the open field to dance away. It was a spontaneous burst of energy inspired by the lone nut but made possible by the first follower.

Our research suggests that once there are three, or as we call it, the *power of three*, the environment is safe enough for voices to be heard and change to occur. Once the lone nut was surrounded not just by the first follower but by the second follower, there were three people up and dancing. The power of three in a team or a work group provides safety and enough support for each other that they can express their points of view in a constructive manner. As pressure mounts on boards of directors to become more diverse, there is a school of thought that gender and racial diversity on boards is imperative. Some proposals call for boards to have at least 40 percent gender diversity. Behind this research is the data that support the concept of the power of three and how it enables individuals to gain confidence in speaking up with opposing positions or points of view.

Why is it that followership has such a bad stigma in our society? In religious context, followership is worthy. Such was the case for the followers of Moses or Jesus. These followers believed in their leaders. They willingly chose to follow them. They trusted that these leaders had their best interests in mind and that they were there to serve them. The leaders showed their followers a better way to live. The leaders had a positive vision for the future and influenced their followers to take positive action to achieve the desired end state. Following is a basic human behavior, but courageous following is more difficult and can be developed.

Why do we follow? There are several reasons we may find ourselves following someone or something. Generally, as followers we are either obligated, compelled, or inspired. Obligatory followership comes into play in many aspects of our life, such as following traffic regulations, instructions from a teacher, visits to the DMV, and the like. Inspirational followership exists when we follow the purpose of an organization or our inner motives to take action. We may not be following the leader, but the cause the individual is trying to achieve.

One of the common themes from Amplifiers I've encountered over the years is how they frame their strategy and decision-making to support a greater purpose. Ann-Marie Campbell, executive vice president of U.S. Stores and International Operations at The Home Depot, advocates for "purpose over titles." She favors purpose first, then position. If a customer needs something in the store, the purpose is to help the customer—the titles go out the door. She likens it to servant leadership, that leaders are there to serve the customers and store associates. Furthermore, Campbell dedicates substantial time walking the stores to better understand the consumer needs as well as those of The Home Depot associates on the front lines. By doing this, she is able to best understand the market that supports her decision-making, but more importantly, she scouts talent to find exemplary followers and future leaders of action and purpose.

The definition of followership is broken into three levels:

- **The capacity or willingness to follow a leader.** This is the most common definition and applies in the broadest setting.
- **An individual who possesses the attributes of positive, active, and independent thinking; who evaluates actions and decisions as opposed to blindly accepting them; and who can succeed and lead others to success without the presence of the leader.** We see this level of followership in many settings, including professional, societal, political, and personal.[1]
- **An interactive role individuals play that complements the leadership role and is equivalent to it in importance for achieving group and organizational performance.** If you look over your life in professional and nonprofessional settings, review some of the most effective leaders and consider who were in their inner circle, chances are there were a few highly trusted people who had the ear of the leader and made them better. They had the courage to speak up, course correct the leader's thinking, and help the organization achieve greater performance.[2]

By definition, leaders need followers. But blind followers, those without the critical thinking required to independently assess what the leaders feed them, may lead to suboptimal outcomes. This is a far too common phenomenon in recent business, political, religious, and social settings. Great leaders grant their followers the right and *obligation* to challenge their point of view. This creates better outcomes, not the other way around. Poor or weak leaders demand compliance to their point of view. They reject outright differing points of view and publicly cast them and the people who profess them aside.

Some might argue that leaders create the vision, set the strategy, and arrange the resources in order for the organization to charge ahead. That is true in part, but I've found that in the most effective organizations, the leader themselves are in fact being led by a core group of trusted followers. This give-and-take dynamic between leader and follower creates the most enduring strategies. The leader needs the humility to accept the input, challenges, and critical adjustments necessary for them to refine the strategy and vision. It is precisely this input from followers that makes success possible.

Organizational culture plays a critical role in understanding followership at a company. For many large global or multinational companies that have been around for decades, there is a whole class of employees that exists just to get by. They have long since discarded their aspirations to ascend the corporate ladder and they have settled into comfortable positions where they have the skills necessary to perform their jobs. Yet there are some companies that have the ability to consistently reinvent themselves and followers in this context may look entirely different.

Robert Kelley published the seminal work on followership in his book, *The Power of Followership*, in 1992. In it, he described five core followership styles based on a two-by-two matrix in which the vertical axis is dependent/independent thinking and the horizontal axis is passive/active participation: passive followers, pragmatist followers, conformist followers, alienated followers, and exemplary followers.[3]

Passive followers do as they are told and rarely think critically. If they do, they generally keep it to themselves or share it with friends outside the work environment. Passive followers require consistent direction and oversight, yet they are able to effectively complete their tasks. Employees in this quadrant are commonly referred to as "sheep." This group of followers are unlikely to resist change if the rest of the organization is already moving toward it because they see safety in masses.

The pragmatist followers are mediocre performers, somewhat stronger than the passive followers, but they are politically astute.

This group of employees are considered "survivors" and they are primarily concerned with "what's in it for me." They respond best to incremental improvements, incremental performance measurements, and incremental change. In most organizations, pragmatist followers represent a large proportion of the employee base. They will participate in change or transformation efforts after they know it is safe to do so. They generally hold key mid-level manager roles and are respected for their subject matter expertise. Pragmatist followers fully meet the expectations of leaders.

Let's look at the conformist followers. Generally speaking, there are more employees in this quadrant than there are in the alienated follower's quadrant. They represent the largest opportunity for leaders to effectuate change. These followers participate but they don't provide healthy criticism. They can be viewed as "yes" people. In big companies that have been successful over the years, many generally have a "nice" culture. The people tend to be cordial and have kind words to say. However safe it may seem, confronting the brutal facts is necessary for organizations to be better. Conformist followers exemplify nice at the cost of being most effective.

Regarding conformist followers, Caulkins shared a story about one of his long-time mentees who was promoted behind him in many roles. Despite being a highly effective executive, his mentee was held back from reaching peak potential because they lacked the necessary follower trait of critical thinking. The mentee was an outstanding order taker, who would frequently say, "I'll do what you want me to do, just let me know." Caulkins emphasized that's not why they were promoted into the role. The mentee was encouraged to think independently so as to be able to present up what he felt was best for the function. If the leader constantly tells the follower what to do, the leader is not only doing his own job but the job of the follower. This follower always worried about what Caulkins thought of him, not applying the critical thinking necessary to advocate for change in order to create greater business performance.

Alienated followers present particular challenges to leaders. They possess the independent and critical thinking necessary to be exemplary followers, but they do not channel this into active participation with the leadership. This group of employees are cynical but talented. One of the key challenges with this set of followers is that they generally have a following of their own due to their ability to think independently and their high level of capability. They may sit through a meeting in seeming agreement, then leave and assert that everything said in the meeting was off base and persuade the group to continue doing as they were. As such, there is a risk that alienated followers may lead others down the wrong path. Leaders need to either quickly convert alienated followers or remove them from the organization.

Over the countless interactions I've had with leaders and Amplifiers across a wide variety of size and complexity of organizations, one common theme has been the disappointment of conformist followers and the anger generated from the alienated followers. Passive and pragmatist followers don't elicit the same level of reaction that ignites the passion of leaders. I think it is because followers offer the greatest potential to change the trajectory or influence the organization's culture.

Alienated followers are critical and independent thinkers. They represent a smaller population within an organization because they have a tendency to self-select and leave the organization resulting in higher turnover. In my interactions with leaders across a wide variety of companies, I marvel at the optimism leaders have that they will be able to convert alienated followers into exemplary followers. Oftentimes, I wonder why the executives put up with alienated follower behavior. But because they are highly capable, and generally outperform the duties and responsibilities of their particular job role, their attitude is overlooked.

Being an exemplary follower is a prerequisite to becoming an Amplifier. These followers are a special breed of employee who seem to accomplish the impossible within organizations. They have a unique blend of independent and critical thinking combined with active participation to drive results. It is not difficult to spot an exemplary follower because they are often out front taking initiative, speaking or acting on behalf of leaders, are extremely competent in their job functions, and are adept at creatively solving problems facing the team or function. What's more, exemplary followers are those individuals who have the courage to speak truth to power—to tell the leaders when they are off track or making the wrong decision—but are able to do it in a constructive manner. In return, they earn the trust and respect of other leaders and their colleagues because their intentions are true, and their actions match the values of the organization.

Dan Caulkins shared an experience when he was an exemplary follower, working for a terrible boss who lacked even the basic leadership skills. Caulkins was out west, somewhat distanced from the New Jersey headquarters and therefore could be considered an absentee boss. Many of Caulkins's peers who also reported to this boss had similar frustrations with the non-responsiveness. Instead of complaining, as a true Amplifier, Caulkins set in motion a strategy to fill the leadership gap in a proactive way, clearly describing the decisions he would be making in the following week and why. He would follow that up with the decisions he made and the decisions he would be making in the subsequent week. He did not let the dysfunction of his boss slow down his need to grow the region. His peers were amazed how he could continue to execute the strategy and carry on in the absence of the decision-maker who was thought to be crucial for success.

When spotting leaders and followers, Tim Hassinger shared an experience with me that he learned in China. When you don't know the language, you learn to watch body language to identify leadership. Oftentimes, body language will give you many clues as to who commands leadership respect within a group. When observing a group of peers, notice when someone talks if the others take their phone out or if they sit upright. By observing, you can see who is really respected and who is ignored.

Effective leaders have a good understanding of what's in the minds and the inner psyche of their followers. These business leaders have invested in the tools to uncover and discover the styles, motives, and traits of the people in the organization. When these are understood in conjunction with performance measures, the full potential of the workforce is uncovered. With this information, the organization can ensure that the best possible people are assigned to the highest impact work. It's important to remember that followers are not cube dwellers. They are out and about throughout the organization and engaging in challenging ways. When reviewing the performance of these followers, there needs to be a core understanding of what makes an exemplary follower—and a sincere desire to extend beyond your core group to find others who fit the bill.

Leadership Lessons: The Power of Three

At Clarkston Consulting, we operate as a group of partners who serve our clients, and we have broad autonomy to do so, as long as the partner remains consistent with our strategy and values. Some of our partners and senior practitioners have developed innovative approaches to solving our clients' needs and have developed new solution offerings that would be beneficial for a number of our clients. Despite how effective these solutions are, I have witnessed how difficult it is for them to influence other partners to bring the same highly effective offerings to their own clients. Generally, a second partner will deliver the solution (perhaps in coordination with the original innovation team) but even after a second client success story, the solution often fizzles out. It's not until a third partner gets involved in delivery, and the magic of the power of three kicks, in where the service offering gains traction in the marketplace. This highlights the power of followership and the importance of not just one but two followers needed to create a safe environment for others to participate.

Over the years, I've watched outstanding performers get drowned out by others in the room. It may be that some of the individuals were more charismatic and always needed to voice their strong opinions first. In some cases, it was due to a lack of gender or racial diversity. When others talked over them, although they were strong performers, they were simply hesitant to voice their concerns or ideas. Tim Hassinger shared his experience with a critical employee, Mary. She was part of a key team filled with charismatic leaders and followers. However, they talked over her and often missed her critical input at important junctures in the decision-making process. Over time, the team learned they needed her input and, furthermore, they learned that before they made any major decision, they made sure they gathered Mary's input prior to advancing the discussion and decision.

Hassinger, recently retired as CEO, shared a gimmick he used to help effect cultural change. Because the culture at this company was so "nice," they were not making difficult decisions and were unwilling to confront each other during meetings when such decisions needed to be made. So, he ordered toy elephants for each of the conference rooms. The elephants symbolized "the elephant in the room" and were used in meetings to provide safety for people to highlight a norm or previous assumption that no longer held true or that needed to be reevaluated.

Finding and Developing Amplifiers

4

Finding and Developing Leaders, Followers, and Amplifiers

"It is not the critic who counts; not the man who points out how the strong man stumbles, or where the doer of deeds could have done them better. The credit belongs to the man who is actually in the arena, whose face is marred by dust and sweat and blood; who strives valiantly; who errs, who comes short again and again, because there is no effort without error and shortcoming; but who does actually strive to do the deeds; who knows great enthusiasms, the great devotions; who spends himself in a worthy cause; who at the best knows in the end the triumph of high achievement, and who at the worst, if he fails, at least fails while daring greatly, so that his place shall never be with those cold and timid souls who neither know victory nor defeat."

—Theodore Roosevelt

When Doug McMillon started at Walmart at the age of sixteen unloading trucks, it seems unlikely that anyone in the Walmart chain of command saw him as the future CEO.[1] Of course, very few entry-level employees will work their way up to the top spot at a company, but how many are passed up because nobody takes the time to better understand the true potential of these individuals?

The best leaders invest in talent. This is one of the greatest responsibilities that leaders have. They commit professionally and personally to developing their followers, and the followers that invest in their own development get the most attention. Leaders need to take the first step and invite their followers to participate in the leader's own development. Amplifiers report that those leaders who are patient teachers, have skin in the game, foster a sense of mutual trust, and make them feel valued are the leaders who make the most lasting impact on the Amplifier's career.

Our experience working with great companies and exceptional leaders has highlighted various character traits, operating styles, and motives of leaders, the combination of which creates the unique fingerprint of each leader and the organizations they shepherd. In the previous section, we dug deeper into what sets apart leaders, executives (or bosses), followers, and subordinates. We followed that up with a review of leadership, followership, and Amplifiers. We contrasted them with management, titled executives, bosses, and subordinates in order to tease out the differences and separate the aspects that differentiate exceptional companies and their top performers. We also identified a long list of character traits, took a fresh look at operating styles, and evaluated the motives behind the high-performing professionals we see in action. By design, the list is longer than it should be, but it is illustrative of a set of character traits, like muscles, that can be strengthened with exercise. In order for anyone to magnify their strengths and shore up their weaknesses, they need to gain a sense of awareness and true critique of where they stand today.

Being a leader means influencing others. Every leader, or boss for that matter, is a teacher. These leaders are either teaching what *to* do or what *not to* do. People throughout the organization study the behavior of leaders. True Amplifiers are the best students of leadership behavior. It is not a casual course for them to take. These Amplifiers are in fact on a PhD journey.

Hassinger shared with me a story of his development journey. He was flying back from a trip to Asia—one of those trips where the flight lasts forever after a grueling week, and although he was completely exhausted, he couldn't sleep. As he was reflecting on the progress his team was making in Asia and thinking back over his career, Hassinger jotted down on paper every one of his leaders into three buckets. The first bucket was the managers no one ever wishes they had. The second bucket contained managers who taught skills and were good examples. This category plays a critical role in talent development, because skills need to be taught in order to develop employees to most effectively get the job done and carry out the mission of the organization. This was a really long list. The third bucket was higher up on the impact to his career and, frankly, how he hoped he had affected others. The key difference in this third bucket was that they cared—they genuinely cared about him and his family. They took a special interest in his development, both as a professional and as an individual.

Early in his career, Tim Hassinger worked for Jim Theis, one of his toughest managers. Theis was the VP overseeing the entire function and had a reputation throughout the organization as a no BS, highly demanding manager. But Theis ended up being one of Hassinger's best managers. When Hassinger was assigned to the department under Theis, he was new to the functional area and his learning curve was straight up. Theis knew this, understood his potential, and immediately set into motion with Hassinger's immediate manager a strategy to ensure his development.

The company had just completed a massive multibillion-dollar joint venture and it was just starting to put in place its leadership development program. It was in the early stages of formation and there was only rough scaffolding in place. The executives knew that they needed to rotate junior talent through key parts of the organization so that they could broaden their skill sets and learn other critical business functions. This ensured that as they progressed up the corporate ladder, they would be more effective at their jobs. After some time, Theis came to Hassinger and delivered this frank message: "I have a good understanding of the next job you'll be in position for and you're not ready. Every week we are going to sit down and review one aspect of the job and go through it in detail in order for you to be prepared to take on that new role and responsibilities."

When Hassinger was promoted to that next job, it was one of the smoothest transitions he had ever had.

Great leaders genuinely care about their followers. They take particular interest in one or more aspects of their lives beyond their professional responsibilities. Bosses with high self-interest do not endear themselves to followers. In these circumstances, followers may learn particular job skills or methods to be more effective managers. Ann-Marie Campbell shared a story about her very early years at The Home Depot. While working as a cashier one day, she saw a crowd of executives doing a store walk through and proactively joined the conversation out of curiosity. One of the executives, Lynn Martineau, asked a question. When no one answered, Campbell stepped up and answered his question, and then returned to her register. Impressed with her willingness to speak up and the content of her response, Martineau made a note to watch out for Campbell. Over the next several decades, he invested in her development as she succeeded in various roles over her career. With every promotion, she credited Martineau as a key driver of her career success, having believed in her even more than she believed in herself.

Even if they do not directly teach, leaders instruct by modeling their behaviors. True followers are sponges and absorb this model behavior. Many leaders fail to realize that what they are doing when they think people are not watching is just as important as what they're doing when they know people are watching. What they say is just as important as what they don't say.

Another aspect of Amplifiers emphasized by Helena Foulkes is the concept of "leading across boundaries," especially as leaders advance their careers in large organizations. The best leaders she's encountered have been able to lead up, down, across, and sideways. One of her mentors was Tom Ryan, who was the CEO at CVS for two-thirds of her career. He inspired, challenged, and trusted her. In many roles, she was the only woman in a particular team or function. Ryan made it safe for her to express her opinion or different point of view on a particular approach.

Over the years, I have witnessed leaders advance to new positions and bring along the followers who have helped them achieve their success. These followers in turn bring along their followers. Leaders and followers possess this symbiotic relationship—it produces a special kind of energy from which they both draw strength and power. Several years ago, I was working closely with the CEO of a major contract research organization serving the biopharmaceutical industry. Although he is a bit older than I am, we both started our careers at the same consulting firm, working for the same partner. It was amazing that as we shared stories about our mutual mentor, we quickly identified how his positive habits left a lasting impression on us several decades later. We reflected on the lessons we had learned from him and what we, in turn, have tried to pass on to our followers. Early in our careers, we are learners and take more than we are able to give. Later in our careers, we are in a position to share a richer set of experiences and perspectives. We become givers rather than takers.

Any company that wants to develop its leaders needs to have a clear understanding of the leadership traits that are most important to the company and a strategy to develop its professionals. There are far more leadership traits being touted in the marketplace that companies should prioritize in their professional development programs. Leaders don't just fall out of trees; leadership requires a special combination of natural talent and nurtured development. In our consulting firm, most of the leadership we need to develop and display for our clients does not come from position power, but from true leadership and influence capabilities. Therefore, our leadership development programs focus primarily on developing leadership traits where position power does not exist. As consultants, it is critical that we get this right, for we achieve results through influence, not by issuing orders.

All organizations have leaders throughout their ranks, but leaders can lead the organization down the wrong path, as we have seen in the news regarding the emissions scandal at Volkswagen and the fatal consequences with Boeing's 737 Max. John Stumpf at Wells Fargo has denied wrongdoing or actual knowledge of what was going on with the fraudulent account opening scandal. As unlikely as that is, and we give him the benefit of the doubt, that means that the follower leaders under him at various levels led the Wells Fargo employees at the branches to pursue their illicit behavior. The challenge is to ensure that the leaders throughout the organization are pursuing the company's mission in an ethical and productive manner. This is where the interplay among leadership, followership, and Amplifiers comes to life.

In his book *Moneyball*, Michael Lewis highlighted a new use of data science and analytics to identify the most impactful traits of baseball prospects for the Oakland Athletics organization. Companies who wish to identify top talent should take a page out of Lewis's book by professionalizing their "scouting" skills. I have never seen this "talent scout" role specifically created within any of the companies with which I've worked over the years. Recruiters and training managers possess some scouting skills, and most managers use these skills when evaluating talent internally. However, as a stand-alone job, the professional talent scout for internal development doesn't seem to exist in corporate America.

When companies do scout for talent, they only seem to do it for leaders. Only leadership development gets the time of day. There is an enormous need to scout for talented followers. Even more fruitful would be to scout for Amplifiers. As emphasized previously in the book, leaders, followers, and Amplifiers exist throughout the rank and file of every organization. Developing a followership development program would yield immediate results. Draw the line where you like: for everyone below the CEO, the CEO's direct reports, or those reporting to the direct reports. All of them would benefit by being a better follower. However, until the term *follower* is destigmatized, there will be little energy to pursue a followership development program. This is an unfortunate outcome. There are so many talented employees who can contribute to the success of the company in an outsized fashion, even if they don't rise to the top ranks of "leadership."

Spotting talent and nurturing talent is not easy to do. Finding and nurturing true Amplifiers is an even bigger challenge. Of the leaders I've encountered over the years and those interviewed for this book, I asked a simple question, "When did you know in your career that the top spot was within your reach?" Not one of them could pinpoint a single point in their careers. I then asked whether or not any of their leaders had ever taken them aside when they were early in their careers to tell them they have the potential to reach the top. Dan Caulkins, the current president and CEO of Benjamin Moore & Co., began his career as a sales correspondent. Corporate culture plays a key role in Amplifier development. Companies that have a long history, and a relatively stable product or service portfolio, tend to revert to the mean. Essentially employees in these types of companies are not rewarded for stepping out or stretching themselves to innovate. To develop someone like Caulkins, management needed to be able to spot extraordinary talent and create the environment where that talent can be nurtured. Successful organizations are aligned around the common goal of identifying top talent within their organization so that it can be developed. The payoff for attracting, developing, motivating, and retaining the best possible human talent is extraordinary.

Defining Leadership, Followership, and Amplifiers for Your Organization

The first step in finding and developing true Amplifiers is to identify the various styles, motives, and traits that are important to the company. Each company should carefully review the traits that make sense for them in the context of their strategy and culture.

The second step is to set out a clear definition for the leadership, followership, and Amplifier *expectations* you have for the company. This is not a one-size-fits-all proposition. It's critical that each organization understands the expectations it has for its high-potential employees. Although these expectations should transcend business cycles and survive current strategy initiatives, they should also adjust with the changing customer or market dynamics.

In order for a company to evaluate its employees on their leadership or followership qualities, it must first define this set of criteria with an understanding of what good leaders or good followers are for that particular company. The first step is to characterize and prioritize leadership attributes important to the company's success. This is then repeated for followership attributes. Once leadership and followership attributes are understood, the Amplifier attributes can be uncovered. We recommend assembling a small team who possess Amplifier characteristics to create the process and method to best proliferate leadership, followership, and Amplifier skills throughout the company.

We have found in our research that most companies that have leadership development programs conflate the elements of management and leadership. However, developing management skills does not automatically lead to increased leadership skills. As a result, many of the methods used in these leadership development programs are misaligned with their intent. Therefore, the first item of business is to review the leadership traits listed in chapter 6, adding any that are missing but relevant for your company and deleting others that are not. For each trait, carefully review the language that makes sense to the organization, then find examples of the trait in action at varying levels of demonstration (low, medium/at expectation, and high). By doing this, the organization can better understand each of the leadership traits relevant for your company through clear behavioral examples.

The next step is to determine the key followership traits successful employees demonstrate at your company. We have found that followership is underappreciated and underrated within most companies. Most companies expect their employees to display strong followership traits, but they lack any of the infrastructure to track the followership styles, motives, or traits of their employee base. We have provided the following approach to tease out the top followership traits for your company.

Developing good followership skills is different than developing good leadership skills. In chapter 7, we outline various follower-ship styles, motives, and traits. We have found in our research that most companies do not have followership as part of their professional development construct. If they do, they blend characteristics of subordinates, which for reasons we outline in chapter 3, we omit from followership traits. Similar to what we did for leadership traits, the first item of business is to review the followership traits listed in chapter 7, adding any that are missing for your company and deleting others that are not a current emphasis for further development. A successful development program focuses on a handful of traits. For each trait, carefully review the language that makes sense to the organization; then find examples of the trait in action at varying levels of demonstration (low, medium/at expectation, and high). By doing this, the organization can better understand each of the followership traits relevant for your company through clear behavioral examples.

We then match the identified leadership and followership traits to determine the Amplifier traits appropriate for your company. Again, there are sustaining and situational Amplifier traits. Companies like Volkswagen and Wells Fargo have systemic cultural issues that require a more focused approach on developing good followers, and thus good Amplifiers. Once the Amplifier traits are identified, we go through the same process to identify, with examples, what it looks like in practice as demonstrated at a low level, at expectation, and at a high level.

After this work is complete, the organization should have a good representation of what they're looking for with respect to leaders, followers, and Amplifiers. By identifying the low, medium, and high demonstrated actions, the broader organization can do a better job scouting for Amplifiers.

Furthermore, this framework serves as a demonstration to the entire organization of desired behaviors that are expected of all. Individuals who lack leadership or followership traits have a hard time spotting those traits in others. A strong manager with low-level leadership capabilities may not be able to fully appreciate an employee's potential leadership capabilities or perhaps may promote a moderately performing individual who also does not demonstrate leadership skills. This is why developing and communicating specific low/medium/high examples of the traits is so critical. Defining these specific behaviors not only gives managers an objective way to measure their team members but also serves as an opportunity to educate and encourage the manager to demonstrate the same behaviors.

Finding Amplifiers

Finding Amplifiers is much easier once the desired Amplifier traits are clearly defined and articulated throughout the organization. Those Amplifier characteristics are unique and can set those individuals apart from the crowd. But that's not always the case. Far more often than managers care to admit, development is suppressed or goes unnoticed at all levels of the organization. An Amplifier stifled in a position working for a bad manager unable to spot talent may not be noticed in the organization. This presents the company with a double challenge. The first challenge is the ineffective manager and the second is the inability to effectively identify and nurture talent. Both pose significant issues that must be addressed.

The school playground provides fascinating examples of talent selection. We have all experienced the quintessential dodgeball team selection dynamics play out. Typically, the same usual suspects step up as the team leaders, who then pick their team players. It was always interesting to see which individuals were picked first. Most times, the leader's selections were based on the individual's skill level. Other times, interestingly, a more skilled person would be picked further down the list than a player of lesser skill. It wasn't until I was well into my professional career that I came to understand why that phenomenon was playing out. Sometimes, the most skilled player is not the best team member. If the player with the most skill lacks effective leadership or followership skills, that player can actually produce detrimental results for the overall team. This is especially true in business. Many professionals have amazing talent and are brilliant at their craft. Yet they are so self-centered, or short tempered, or stretch ethics, or follow their own plan, that they cannot be relied on to effectively enhance group performance. Their skills are strong enough that they remain employed by the company, but they require extra management and oversight. These individuals should take on roles that channel their expertise as a sole contributor but do not necessarily empower them to lead teams.

There are a number of methods to identify high-potential and rising stars within your workforce:

1. **Selection requests for team participation.** Amplifiers can be identified by understanding and tracking which employees are consistently selected by their leaders for important team assignments—and *why* they were selected. The work that gets done through teams usually requires a high degree of interaction and influence across, throughout, and even outside the organization. As a result, the character traits highlighted for Amplifiers become critical attributes for team member selection. When leaders assemble teams, they look for core subject matter expertise, leadership capabilities, or both. Simply put, leaders want to staff teams with individuals who have the greatest ability to magnify the success of the team. Although employees with strong subject matter expertise with limited leadership potential are still key contributors to these teams, it is the Amplifiers who determine if a project is wildly successful. Tracking who and why employees are selected—or not selected—by their leaders and peers for important assignments can be one way to identify those individuals who are recognized as Amplifiers in the organization.

   However, just because an individual is selected for a team assignment may not always indicate that they are in fact Amplifiers. Over the years, we have played a role in selecting the individuals who will serve on our clients' project teams and we always demand the best people. Almost always, our clients affirmatively confirm that they have selected only their top-performing employees to staff these projects. However, at least half the time, it becomes painfully clear that either the leaders knowingly did not do so or, as is more often the case, the leaders had misjudged the performance potential of the assigned team members. It is therefore critical to understand and verify why an individual was selected for the team to better predict how they will perform on that team.

2. **Formal performance reviews.** Most companies have formal performance reviews with regularly scheduled checkpoints with their managers. Performance criteria is usually focused on the elements of job performance necessary to complete the activities to achieve the predetermined goals and objectives of the role. Some companies also evaluate the individual's contributions that are above and beyond their core job description, such as participating in recruiting, training, or thought leadership efforts. Performance criteria may also consider how the employee conducts themselves with respect to the company's core values or even specifically assess their leadership potential. Companies can adapt these tools and processes to identify Amplifiers based on the identified Amplifier traits.

Companies that capture a leadership development pipeline would be well served to broaden their evaluation criteria to include followership traits and, more importantly, Amplifier traits. It is very difficult to become a successful leader without being a true Amplifier. Companies that emphasize only leadership traits and fail to evaluate Amplifier traits may risk promoting employees into leadership positions who lack the corresponding skills to be successful. An example of this is Robert Nardelli, who had a successful career at GE, a company well known for its robust leadership development process. Nardelli rose to the highest levels at the company, including being one of three considered for CEO succession. However, having not developed Amplifier traits during his career, his role as The Home Depot's CEO earned him Condé Nast Portfolio's ranking as one of the "Worst American CEO's of All Time" due to his autocratic management style, relentless cost cutting at the expense of top talent in the organization, and the resulting alienation of investors and the board.[2]

3. **Volunteering and hand raising.** Amplifiers are driven to contribute and consistently raise their hands and volunteer for additional assignments. I've always been impressed when I see team members step up to help when a company is facing a particularly thorny challenge. Amplifiers proactively tackle issues within their department or function, but many times, they reach out cross-functionally to support another team or executive. These employees already have a full plate, yet they know they can make a difference and help to solve the problem. Amplifiers demonstrate a level of initiative and confidence necessary for success in multiple areas of the organization. Companies that capture specifics about how and where all employees are delivering above and beyond have a tendency to identify more exemplary followers and true Amplifiers.

Many times, initiatives seem to be led by a handful of the same people. On the one hand, this is good in that these individuals are typically trusted, have a proven track record of success, and are able to influence others to contribute. Noticing and recognizing the people leading these initiatives is crucial to set a positive example for others to do the same. But companies risk discouraging others from stepping forward by constantly nominating the same people for high-profile opportunities. Good leaders identify employees who are stepping forward in smaller settings and position them for some of these more high-profile opportunities. By casting a wider net, companies will expose more employees to the broad employee population and create more change agents.

Another important indicator of Amplifiers can be seen by tracking those individuals who are more likely to attract followers and are voluntarily willing to serve. Employees may seek out specific leaders for whom they want to work, demonstrating the magnetism of these leaders and their ability to engage a broad group of followers. When followers consistently choose to work with certain leaders, it is a good indication that the leader is also an Amplifier. Capturing the sought-after status of leaders and followers enables the company to channel that information to understand leadership and followership behaviors and the people who possess them.

We have seen the unconscious selection bias used by leaders to pick their teams. In Clarkston's Diversity Equity and Inclusion consulting practice, we ask workshop participants to list their "trusted ten"—those ten individuals in their lives that they trust the most. This exercise often highlights the lack of diversity of an individual's inner circle, which can be replicated in the leader's selection of team members. Leaders must be more intentional about expanding their circle of trusted advisors. Doing so is an excellent way to lead by example from the top, enabling this practice to cascade down to their followers. For companies to make sustainable change in the diversity of their teams, they need to analyze team selection behaviors to ensure that the company is finding Amplifiers.

Developing Amplifiers

True Amplifiers are lifelong learners. They are constantly seeking opportunities for informal or formal professional development. Amplifiers are students of leaders and followers alike and are constantly calibrating those lessons into their own behavior. Although they are self-motivated, focused efforts to develop Amplifiers will produce meaningful results. Developing Amplifiers is one of the most important activities a company can pursue. By investing in the styles, traits, and behaviors necessary to build Amplifiers in the company, the culture will be strengthened and will magnify the power of teams to produce outsized performance.

Effects require causes. If a baker wants a chocolate cake, they need to collect the necessary ingredients and follow the directions. If they do, a chocolate cake will emerge. Replacing strawberry for the chocolate will not produce the same result. The same is true for creating Amplifiers. Defining and promoting the traits and demonstrated behaviors of leaders, followers, and Amplifiers serve as the basis for developing the traits necessary to build Amplifiers.

Using these styles, motives, and traits, companies can plot their employees in the matrix shown in Figure 4.1. This matrix highlights the development needs for employees in each category. Every successful company will have employees that occupy each of the five boxes. The focus should be centered on developing more Amplifiers. It is important to note that such an assessment is relevant only at a given point in time. Ideally, companies will continuously update this assessment so that an employee's progression to Amplifier can be tracked and understood. For example, if an employee has moved from one of the quadrants into the common core in the middle, the development necessary to bring them to the Amplifier quadrant may require a different path.

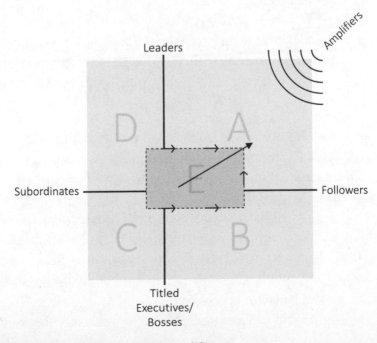

FIGURE 4.1 Developing Amplifiers

The first step in developing Amplifiers is understanding where employees fit in Figure 4.1. There are five categories of employees:

- Employees in quadrant A are Amplifiers, those high-impact employees who display the unique combination of strong leadership and strong followership skills.
- Employees in quadrant B possess some or all of the followership skills important to the company but they do not have sufficient leadership skills.
- Employees in quadrant C have a low level of leadership skills and a low level of followership skills.
- Employees in quadrant D display greater leadership skills but lack the necessary followership skills.
- Employees that occupy the center of the matrix in box E represent a large percentage of the population within the organization and demonstrate some characteristics of each.

For the purpose of building out development plans, we assume that the employees have the requisite skills and aptitude to carry out the core activities of their job function. For example, a machinist on the production line who is a solid contributor, executes based on instructions provided, and produces work within the specified tolerance of error is still a valued employee even if they exist in quadrant C.

Employees who operate in quadrant B possess some or all of the followership skills important to the company, but they lack leadership skills. Good followers are very valuable in an organization. It is critical to understand the motives of the employees in this quadrant to ensure that they are good candidates for leadership development. Some employees genuinely do not want to take on leadership roles for a whole host of personal and psychological reasons. Some may simply get stressed with the added responsibility and accountability, others are overrun by fear, and still others may have certain personal reasons why they need to take a step back from increasing leadership responsibilities at a particular point in their lives. But nonetheless, these employees can be valuable contributors and amplify certain aspects of the company's culture, strategy, or mission. Understanding motives of employees in this quadrant enables leaders to work with them to grow different leadership skills in a more prescribed or targeted way. Other employees in this quadrant simply have not been exposed to adequate leadership training or may be too inexperienced in their careers to develop robust leadership skills. These employees have the desire but lack the skills. Employees who fit this category are perfect choices to put through structured leadership development programs. By strengthening their leadership skills, they will be able to further leverage their already strong followership skills to move closer to the Amplifier quadrant.

Employees who operate in quadrant C generally lack both sufficient leadership and followership skills. As mentioned, these employees may be highly capable individual performers, hard workers, are reliable, and perform their work with defects within the acceptable margin. In most organizations, there are many employees who fit this category. They are necessary to accomplish many of the routine tasks, frontline production or distribution, or may even occupy some knowledge worker positions. However, all companies will benefit by helping these quadrant C employees migrate toward quadrant B or E. By teaching these employees greater followership skills, they can begin to improve their critical and independent thinking, gain the courage to challenge, or develop other traits that are demonstrated by strong followers. Most companies prioritize leadership development programs for a select few and do not make them widely available for the broader employee base, especially individuals who are currently residing in quadrant C. Generally speaking, allocating resources to obtain the best and highest return is wise but there are ways to boost their performance outside of formal development programs. Focusing on followership skills first for these employees will create immediate payback, and as they successfully develop followership skills, they can become better candidates for leadership development investment.

Employees in quadrant D are the riskiest group of employees at the company. They possess leadership skills but lack the essential followership skills to ensure they lead their followers consistent with the organization's strategy. When leaders lead groups of companies down the wrong path, either directly or by example, they are cancer cells that the organization must extract. We have seen high-profile examples of this, such as Andy Fastow, the CFO of Enron under CEO Jeffrey Skilling. In that case, the individuals perpetrating fraud were so senior in the organization that only the board could have taken action to fire them. Luckily, some good followers emerged as whistle-blowers, which helped to uncover the massive fraud. Leaders in this quadrant yield power and influence, yet they may have bad motives or bad intent. Employees without sufficient positive role models are susceptible to follow these leaders down the wrong path, becoming "disillusioned renegades." For employees filling rank-and-file management positions who are in this quadrant, investing in developing stronger followership skills is a necessity. This should not be viewed as optional training for these employees. It is critical that the organization gains alignment and develops critical followership skills necessary to carry out its mission.

Employees who operate in the center of the matrix in box E are a relatively large group of generally well-aligned and engaged employees. Again, improving followership skills first, then leadership skills, will provide a significant return on investment. Employees in this quadrant need to be brought to a higher level of followership or they risk becoming the disillusioned renegades. As these followership skills are developed, these employees become excellent candidates for leadership development opportunities. The return on investment is the highest for followership and leadership development for employees who operate in this quadrant because they already possess a foundational level of both skills.

Developing Amplifier Skills

The path to developing true Amplifiers in your organization is only possible if there is effective followership along with promising leadership skills. And we have found that being a strong leader requires being a good follower first. Therefore, our recommendation is to focus on building a robust followership program and merge it with leadership development programs that are already in flight. This is the fastest path toward building the Amplifier skills necessary for great leaders to magnify the power of their teams.

Developing followership skills is a journey that takes practice and good mentorship. Great leaders are engaged in developing people, and they especially enjoy developing exemplary followers. Building good followership skills requires a similar approach to building leadership skills but flexes different muscles. And similar to leadership development programs, the best followership development programs are framed as a series of trait development, style analysis, and application-based learning exercises.

Case Study on Amplifier Development

An effective Amplifier development program incorporates the key elements of followership and Amplifier traits into a comprehensive interactive program. We found that people learn best in learning pods, such as running clubs or book clubs, where like-minded individuals get together and learn from each other. We layer in the elements of apprenticeship from experienced professionals teaching those with less experience. This interactive method produces extraordinary results.

Amplifier Trait	Explanation	High (*Always Exhibits*)
Authentic	Consistently sticks to their ideals and is willing to speak truth to power	• Able to speak up in group or individual settings to represent their authentic point of view and opinion regardless of the topic • Recognizes they don't know all the answers and openly taps colleagues with the knowledge to engage in the solutions or provide the information • Admits mistakes and gives credit • Reliable to deliver on their word/promises • Encourages colleagues to be their authentic self, bringing their whole self to work and appreciating others for who they are
Consigliere	Represents the followers' perspectives and advises the leader to make more informed, inclusive, insightful, risk-adjusted, and impactful decisions	• Is willing to stick their neck out to take on the risk of a delivering difficult messages to the leader on behalf of followers • Challenges preliminary thoughts and decisions a leader is considering, seeking insights from core stakeholders, and drives better decision-making processes • Respects the privacy and discretion of conversations with leaders and followers as they bridge the gap

Amplifier Trait	Explanation	High (Always Exhibits)
Courageous	Takes the right course of action regardless of popularity or consensus, regardless of personal or professional risk	• Shows the courage to speak truth to power, to tell leadership and other stakeholders when they are wrong or off course without fear of reprisal • Proactively shares the right but unpopular message with leaders and other followers despite possible repercussions • Seeks out challenges for themselves and their teams and is willing to take on risk for an appropriate level of gain • Embraces new or difficult assignments with a learning and growth mindset • Proactively presents ideas instead of waiting to be asked

(continued)

Amplifier Trait	Explanation	High (Always Exhibits)
Empowering	Encourages others to act, shares/grants responsibility and account-ability, communicates expectations, and actively works to create an environment where one can be successful	• Grants the power and authority to their teams or followers to lead autonomously and provide them with the opportunity to be creative in their solution or approach • Proactively provides guidance or direction to any team member when it is needed or requested (when applicable) • Accepts accountability for the quality and final outcome of work • Consistently recognizes team members for their contributions privately and publicly • Expects followers to stretch themselves, but provides a safety net if they begin to falter

Amplifier Trait	Explanation	High (*Always Exhibits*)
Followership	Possesses the attributes of a positive, active, and independent thinker who evaluates actions/ decisions as opposed to blindly accepting them; can succeed without the presence of a leader; fills in leadership gaps when they exist	• Exerts influence on the leader in a confident and unemotional manner to help the leader avoid costly mistakes • Speaks truth to power in an effective and constructive manner; knows not only when to disagree with the leader but also how to do so without being disagreeable • Reliably assumes responsibility for a group or team, enabling the leader to increase leverage • Shows diplomacy when voicing differences of opinions in a constructive and tactful manner and ultimately supports the group's decisions • Embraces change and acts as an effective change agent • Is loyal to the organization, team, and partner in success and takes satisfaction in the leader's success • Displays the judgment to know the difference between a directive that a leader gives on how to proceed that they do not agree with and a directive that is wrong

(continued)

Amplifier Trait	Explanation	High (*Always Exhibits*)
Inclusive	Cultivates a professional environment in which all individuals are treated fairly, respectfully, and have equal access to opportunities and resources	• Deploys the power of three when forming strategic teams or departments or business functions • Seeks out diversity of experience, perspectives, and representation to inform decisions and actions • Creates a safe space and invites underrepresented voices to be heard in team and individual settings • Fosters true collaboration that appreciates the uniqueness of each team member's contributions to drive success • Speaks up when others are being excluded or marginalized; challenges to ensure proper representation • Possesses a keen awareness of cultural differences, language, and phraseology to build a climate of trust • Remains aware of conscious and unconscious bias and actively combats it • Avoids favoritism in communication, selection, and involvement

Amplifier Trait	Explanation	High (*Always Exhibits*)
Magnetic	Attracts leaders and followers alike to invest and collaborate with them to magnify the power of teams and the organization	• Displays the ability to influence and bring together leaders and followers alike into a common direction and alignment • Articulates the vision, plan, and rationale to accomplish challenging and worthwhile endeavors, large or small • Shows sincerity and genuine care for others' well-being • Invests in coaching and mentoring team members of all levels and expects others to do the same • Embodies a leader that individuals would follow into a burning building
Mindful	Exemplifies a true understanding of their surroundings, mindset of stakeholders, corporate environment; demonstrates high emotional intelligence	• Possesses a conscious sense of the current surroundings with a keen sense of how to acknowledge prevailing circumstances as they actually are and frame decisions accordingly • Articulates a true representation of the strengths and weaknesses as they are, not as leaders want them to be • Has an accurate understanding of the current starting place of the organization and the mindset of the employees • Resolves to advance the cause and the mission of the company

(continued)

Amplifier Trait	Explanation	High (*Always Exhibits*)
Standard setting	Sets higher and more ambitious standards of excellence by example and expects others to grow	• Constantly increases the quality and output of the work product and raises the bar for performance • Is principled in thoughts and actions and incorporates the highest levels of standards and principles into the work • Reinvigorates team performance by painting a vision and corresponding execution plan for a higher level of service, performance, or goals that the team did not think possible to achieve • Reinvents ways of doing business to set new standards of performance
Teacher/student	Displays the characteristics of a life-long teacher and career student	• Possesses a passion for learning new skills and knowledge that can be applied in a practical way to grow the company and the employees • Invests time and energy in developing followers and derives satisfaction from seeing their followers grow their careers • Recognizes how to adapt their learning/teaching style to optimize knowledge acquisition or develop followers

Whether it's Campbell starting as a cashier at The Home Depot, Caulkins as an entry-level sales correspondent at Benjamin Moore & Co., Foulkes a junior marketer at CVS Health, or McMillon unloading trucks at Walmart, the key to these remarkable leaders' ascension to the highest levels has been these outstanding companies' ability to scout and develop talent. Although their companies may not have immediately recognized them as Amplifiers, they knew their styles, motives, and traits were worth developing. As companies formalize their development of Amplifiers, we can expect to see magnified corporate performance and increased impact of the power of teams.

5

Total Talent and Amplifier Cells

There is a famous quote by the management guru Peter Drucker, "Culture eats strategy for breakfast." Drucker's main idea is that regardless of your corporate strategy, it is the human element that makes or breaks corporate performance. Further, according to Ken Andrews, the actions a company takes tells more about its strategy than what it says.[1] Companies spend an enormous amount of time and money building new strategies and managing them with the intent of achieving their stated goals. Yet the heartbeat of great corporate performance consists of the individual human capital deployed to bring the strategy to life. Great companies invest in their people and their culture.

The most successful organizations look beyond the culture within their four walls and consider all the human talent that must come together in order to execute their purpose and mission. Culture is being defined on a broader scale to include the entire ecosystem comprehensive of all human talent, whether employed full-time or not. These top-performing companies analyze not just their own talent but also their contingent talent, business partners, and influencers who help bring strategy to life. Leaders and successful companies analyze their portfolios of talent holistically similar to how the top investment portfolio fund managers evaluate their proper investment mix. Consider this: companies rely on external human capital for critical functions in marketing, legal, audit and tax, transformation consulting, technology consulting, contract manufacturing, clinical trial management, and other essential knowledge workers. It is critical to incorporate a total talent strategy as part of corporate strategy.

Scope of Talent

When pressed, most executives understate the level of full-time equivalent employees who are working on their behalf. Stated head count numbers are significantly below the total head count required for most organizations to deliver on their mission. Take Apple for example. Apple clearly understands its impact on employment and job creation globally. According to Apple's website and investor relations pages and securities filings,[2] Apple has a stated head count of 147,000 full-time employees. For now, they contract manufacture the chip technology used inside their devices, which likely requires many more hundreds of thousands of workers. They contract manufacture the devices as well. The Foxconn manufacturing facility in Zhengzhou, China, known as "iPhone City," is said to have as many as 350,000 workers.[3] In addition, Apple has a robust iOS and App Store ecosystem that according to its estimate accounts for 2.1 million jobs. In total, Apple claims that it is responsible for 2.7 million jobs in the US and abroad. Apple's consumers care about how Apple treats all the people who are part of its employment ecosystem, whether or not they are full-time employees. Apple cares about the culture of its extended iOS workforce, which is nearly ten times larger than its own employment base, and accounts for 22 percent, or $64 billion, of its $294 billion total revenue.[4]

Another example of organizations that place significant value on their total talent strategy are major apparel makers. Many of them subcontract the creation of their garments to lower-cost parts of the world. In the past, inhumane conditions were commonplace in garment factories in remote parts of the world. However, garment companies have paid more attention to the working conditions their contract manufacturers deploy while making their products. This new focus on total organizational culture was driven by the significant brand hit that many companies took as a result of the stories of local abusive practices hitting the press. Leaders in these companies can no longer afford to ignore how their contract manufacturers treat their workers. The culture of the brand carries through and into the culture of its contract manufacturers. More and more, consumers care about how companies treat their employees, and they dole out rewards and punishments to these companies through the choices they make with the dollars they spend. Similarly, investors are making statements through their investment decisions, as demonstrated by the rise of environmental, social, and governance investing, which is catching on and gaining favor as a key area of focus across several major investor categories.

Although placing a deeper scrutiny on the working conditions of these factories has become a trend, there are still companies seeking to do business with corrupt factories. The willingness to turn a blind eye is largely driven by a focus on profitability at all costs, typically led by supply chain or procurement functions. Rarely do we see significant involvement of the HR organization, even though they are best equipped to understand corporate culture and the human competencies necessary to manage such a vast workforce.

One of the most baffling practices that is so common among many of the Fortune 1000 organizations is the delegation of acquiring and contracting human talent to a purchasing department. These companies contract consulting and other temporary labor as if they are buying pens, pencils, or widgets. Purchasing is far more concerned with rates and terms than they are with identifying and selecting top talent who can amplify their transformation efforts or supplement their teams. Engaging outside talent that is capable of working well with internal employees within the preexisting organizational culture is far more nuanced and requires different skills. HR does not turn to purchasing to recruit new employees or negotiate inbound salaries. Companies are on the wrong end of accumulating the best contingent talent to enhance their strategies. If culture trumps strategy, one of the most important elements is how the culture of this external human capital integrates with corporate culture. Obviously, purchasing skills are critical in order to obtain the best possible terms for the company. But oftentimes they dominate the process, and companies lose sight of the forest through the trees.

Over the years, we have been brought in to clean up projects for some very large and sophisticated global companies that have failed to deliver one or more aspects of their transformation projects. This outcome is most commonly the result of "low-cost" bidding for projects that are dependent on humans, not only to deliver the project but also to engage with the company in an integrated and holistic manner, bringing together collective talents from across the company. We call these types of projects our "extreme project makeovers." Almost every time there is failure, it is not because of inadequate technology or a misaligned strategic vision, but rather it has boiled down to not having assembled the right human capital—internal and external.

As the tasks that knowledge workers perform for companies increases, so too does the need for elevating HR's role in ensuring that all the talent being deployed to enable corporate strategy is aligned with the culture that a company is trying to achieve. Many companies already have HR business partners assigned to the different functional units or departments within the company. However, their scope typically just involves full-time employees. This is a strategic mistake. Most transformation efforts fail. The root cause is usually not because the strategic intent is wrong, but because of the human capital assigned to do the work. There are several key procurement and HR activities for effective decisions about total human capital so that the organization can fully realize its strategic objectives. There are usually at least three key groups that need to collaborate to acquire outside contract human resources talent: the business function, HR, and procurement. The first requirement is to create a detailed job description, list of outcomes, or list of deliverables. Each contract service position, or team of consultants should be vetted to ensure they are qualified to complete the documented tasks required. This is typically a business function. These employees also should be vetted for cultural fit by the HR team. For positions that will be interacting with the company's other employees, they should have a consistent and aligned character and set of core values. Procurement then reviews the contract terms, rates, and competitiveness of the arrangement. The combination of capabilities and cultural fit usually mean the difference between project success or failure. It is one of the key reasons that transformation efforts fail. Making sure these factors are in place is far more important than getting the best rate or payment terms. Procurement can find the lowest cost, but if the outside service firm fails to deliver on the project, their individual rates do not matter.

The Continuum of Talent

Another element of total talent strategy is called the continuum of talent. Total talent begins at the various sources of supply. One of the highest profile examples of talent development is Walmart. Doug McMillon, Walmart's current CEO, began his career as a teenager unloading trucks for an hourly wage. Over his thirty-year career, he has held multiple roles with increasing management and leadership responsibility. Digging deeper into his career, one can see how he has demonstrated the powerful blend of followership and leadership that creates a true Amplifier. Walmart is known for developing its associates. Most of its store managers and corporate executives have held positions in the stores themselves. Walmart is effective at bringing in fresh talent and perspective to round out the skills of its management team. This blend of developing junior talent and injecting it with seasoned talent all within an integrated professional development environment has led to Walmart's phenomenal success.

Companies are increasingly reaching further upstream, and in some cases, even engaging high school students for internships. The war for talent, especially for diverse talent, remains fierce, and companies are becoming far more creative in how they seek to fill their supply funnel. Figure 5.1 demonstrates how leading companies view their total talent, feeder systems, and even alumni. These companies seek to engage people at all levels to unlock the power they bring to create the holistic culture.

Successful companies look at the total scope of talent available to them. As previously noted, the ecosystem of talent surrounding Apple is a ten times order of magnitude ratio of jobs created to people employed by Apple. This example, although magnified in the case of Apple, is not unique. In the biopharmaceutical industry, a similar phenomenon exists. For a drug company to bring a new drug to market, there is an entire ecosystem surrounding the drug. There are contract research organizations that help run and manage the clinical trials. There are contract manufacturing organizations that produce the active ingredients, then fill, pack, and finish the final product. There are the big drug distributors. Some drug companies rely on contract sales organizations. They engage with key opinion leaders to influence physicians to prescribe the drugs. There are consultants engaged for market studies and pricing analysis. And, of course, there are advisors for regulatory affairs. The list goes on. All this human capital needs to come together to coalesce around the common goal of bringing that drug to market. It is the collective sum of all these entities and people within the entities that need to be activated for the strategy and new product introduction to be successful. Great companies understand their cultures and the specific employee profile that will thrive in that culture.

Career employment at a single company is far less common today than it was decades ago. This brings advantages and disadvantages for employees and employers. Technology and availability of information has made it easier for knowledge workers to switch companies while progressing in their careers. Employers benefit from the diversity of thoughts and ideas these new employees bring to them. But they lose cultural consistency and the loyalty effect produced by long-term employees. As the war for talent increases and employees' careers become more tied to their own accomplishments, employees are less likely to choose career employment by a single employer.

FIGURE 5.1 Total Talent Pipeline

There are two types of new recruits, which are depicted on the left side of Figure 5.1. The first type of new recruit is the experienced new hire that companies recruit to fill open positions created either through business growth or to replace a vacancy left by employee departure. Generally speaking, hiring for this type of new recruit is a pretty straightforward process. Job descriptions are built outlining key job competencies, which employers post to cast a net of candidates. The employer then screens for competence and cultural fit. Some companies look for leadership capabilities, but very few screen for the even more important followership capabilities. Without screening for followership capabilities, finding Amplifiers becomes coincidental and not a premeditated and proactive pursuit among recruiters.

The war for top talent starts with entry-level employees. During my consulting career, I have been amazed with the number of companies that do not emphasize matriculating new employees into the fold. Some companies have formal management training programs, and others rely on managers in a particular department or function to develop junior talent through informal mentorship and on-the-job training. However, companies want immediate results. We see these companies leaning too heavily on hiring experienced individuals who require limited training to hit the ground running. Although this may be a necessary strategy for certain roles, the cost per hire is significantly higher. And that higher starting salary is the gift that keeps on giving, as annual pay raises continue to add to that mounting labor cost year after year.

Instead, smart companies take a portfolio approach to their total talent strategy, understanding that the most effective strategy is to have a good mix of experienced talent coupled with a robust feeder system of junior talent. These total talent companies invest in formal training programs to matriculate junior talent into the organization. Integrating junior talent takes time in the short run but has a significant return on investment in the medium and long-term. This approach is often found in professional services businesses, where they are selling the knowledge of their practitioners. The best accounting, legal, consulting, investment banking, and similar services firms all deploy a robust entry-level new hire development and apprentice model. Companies in other industries can and should learn from this example.

Years ago, one of my consulting clients recognized the need to develop a team with a new skill to support the technology implementation we were providing. Despite being a Fortune 50 company, the organization had no formal process to onboard junior talent into the technology group. I recall raising this issue with the chief information officer and the executive sponsor of the project. They asked me to oversee a couple of entry-level college hires and to incorporate them on the project so that they could learn what we were doing and be in a position to provide cost-effective support after the project was completed. We agreed to take them on and helped with the interviews, onboarding, and original training and development. Further, we agreed that for a period of six months, the new hires would work on tasks that were specifically related to their new professional development, as well as others that were tangentially important so they could learn more general business operations. Furthermore, we allowed them to practice their new skills by developing certain components of the system that were less critical for the deployment but enabled them to gain hands-on experience with the internal workings of the system. Everything the new hires worked on was real work of value and served as developmental opportunities in their training journey, each task building on the other. By the end of the onboarding period, the new hires had not only obtained knowledge of the business through their real-world work product but also they had learned enough along the way so that they became highly capable and productive developers, able to support the new technology rollout for the company.

More recently, companies are employing new ways to identify experienced hires, such as evaluating or developing nontraditional candidates for certain roles. For example, with the recent advent of code schools, being a strong web developer or systems engineer no longer requires a four-year college degree. Some companies continue to struggle to fill these hard-to-fill positions because they remain steadfast in old ideals of the target recruit. They need new "Moneyball" metrics to broaden the total available talent at their disposal. Instead, visionary companies are getting creative by leveraging these code schools to transition non-degreed employees, say from customer service to the IT group. These employees have a wealth of knowledge about the company and the customer that they can bring when developing new applications to support the business. Such creativity serves to develop and retain talent and institutional knowledge while enabling these organizations to find hard-to-fill tech talent in a cost-effective manner. Having helped change their career trajectory, these trusted employees are more likely to remain loyal to the organization, creating a truly win-win situation for all.

In the technology space, the cost of talent has skyrocketed, and it is very much a seller's market. Executives who are frustrated with the cost of IT talent should seriously consider these entry-level apprentice development programs. We are currently invested in and working with Momentum Learning, a code school designed to change the career trajectory of lifelong learners by teaching them how to become application developers, web developers, and full stack engineers. Momentum Learning is working with visionary companies who appreciate the need to collaborate to source hard-to-find talent. Momentum works together with these companies to identify candidates for the code school who have the aptitude to learn technology skills and, ultimately, be in a position to be employed by these companies post-certification. By doing this, the companies win and create a loyal band of new employees. Recently, Momentum Learning created a special program for entry-level diverse talent through its Momentum@HBCU code schools.

The middle of the barbell in Figure 5.1 illustrates where companies use direct employees and tap into a vast array of service and contract workers. There are a lot of studies about the cost of replacing employees who leave. This cost is real and companies that focus on employee engagement and culture outperform those that leave these critical corporate dynamics to happenstance. There is far less research on the cost to replace service providers for repetitive services that are provided to these companies. For drug companies, replacing a contract manufacturer of one of their drug products can be an extremely time-consuming and expensive endeavor for many reasons, including regulatory costs. There is a definite trade-off between injecting new and fresh ideas into an organization and the institutional knowledge that service providers have gained over time. Great companies balance these trade-offs and evaluate the service provider's ability to integrate culturally when considering contract renewals and awarding future work.

Another large group of engaged workers, generally not part of the core employee base of the company, are workers in the respective ecosystem of the company. For paint companies, it is the network of corporate or independent painting companies that apply their product by the gallon for the end-use consumer or commercial application.

In Apple's case, it is the ecosystem of application developers selling through the App Store. In other cases, it is the independent workers in the gig economy who might be delivering food, driving passengers, and countless other activities that support companies and their products. These gig economy workers exist completely at arm's length from the companies they support, and the companies themselves have very little control over the culture or the actions these gig workers take on a daily basis. Some experts believe that the world is moving toward the gig economy. Although gig economy workers are surely a component in the overall pie chart distribution of work, for most companies it is more likely they will remain a minority slice of the pie.

The right side of Figure 5.1 identifies alumni and retired workers as assets and sources of valuable information for companies. Great companies who genuinely care about their people would like them to spend their careers at the company, even though, for various reasons, their employees may not always stay through retirement. These companies invest the time and effort to care for these employees beyond the duration for which they are employed. Alumni networks can be a rich source for candidate and sales referrals; they are already equipped to provide a warm introduction. Furthermore, alumni may have additional market insights to share. To capitalize on these opportunities, some companies create formal or informal networks of former employees. Other companies engage their retired workforce as mentors, brand ambassadors, or in other ways to keep them engaged in a mutually beneficial way.

Finally, there are countless other consumers, patients, or other influencers that make a mark on the company and its culture. Successful companies monitor this social channel to capture the current thinking about the company, employees, and its brands. This virtual extension is a source of value for those companies, and many have figured out how to tap into these networks in very creative ways.

One of my favorite examples is the story of Nathan Apodaca.[5] In 2020, the United States was burnt out from the economic fallout of the pandemic and emotionally drained and frustrated by the ongoing examples of racial injustice. Apodaca caught national attention after his car broke down. Instead of a glum attitude, he took to his skateboard in a joyful manner singing to Fleetwood Mac and drinking Ocean Spray. Americans desperately needed the good news story, and his positivity was rewarded when his video went viral. Without even knowing it before it happened, Ocean Spray would see its sales spike and its brand took on a joyful element in a fresh way. This is a valuable illustration of how organizational culture can be affected through direct and indirect means. Companies think they control all the elements that influence their brand and culture, yet a viral video of a joyful Apodaca can have more impact than they could have ever anticipated.

Amplifier Impact on Total Talent

Amplifiers play an outsized role and increase the impact on organizations. They have the ability to magnify the effectiveness of their colleagues, raising underperformers to performers, and encouraging performers to achieve even greater results. Amplifiers have the ability to clearly understand what the leader is seeking to accomplish on the one hand, while reaching back with the other to influence and lead followers down the right path along the journey. By doing this, they impart on their followers the aspects of the corporate culture that cement the bond to create lasting and sustainable performance for the company.

One of the ways Amplifiers affect the culture is through their persistent thirst for knowledge, learning, and growth. Amplifiers establish a culture of mentorship that is pervasive among their colleagues. When interacting with leaders at various levels, one of the common traits we see in Amplifiers is the sense of accomplishment they receive by giving. It's fun to see their eyes light up when they describe a mentee who has done well under their tutelage. Amplifiers take pride in the success and accomplishments of their mentees.

On the flip side, they are also engaged with their mentors by stretching them to be better leaders and helping them achieve their own career successes.

Over time, followers develop into Amplifiers, whose followers then develop their followers into Amplifiers, whose followers then develop their followers into Amplifiers, and so on. It is a chain of leadership-followership like a great-grandparent through the descendant's family tree. This relationship consists of learning and developing hard skills, leadership skills, Amplifier skills, and followership skills, thereby creating a loyal and robust culture that endures over time. As the leaders rise in their careers and take on more leadership responsibility, they pull along their followers, who in turn pull along their followers. As long as they are true Amplifiers and not subordinates tethered to a transient titled executive leader, they will create a powerful team at the top—with succession planning organically built in.

Although there are many benefits of this virtuous positive cycle, my recent work with consistent and equitable career experiences has taught me that unless these "power teams" are inclusive and the circle is widened, they can create negative outcomes by perpetuating the lack of advancement of underrepresented populations within the company. We expand on this in greater detail in chapter 11.

Micro-interactions are great teachers for people who are curious by nature and observant. Great leaders have a sense of awareness and they realize that their micro interactions have the opportunity to make a positive impression on their followers. Amplifiers are keen students and teachers themselves. They are constantly aware and seek opportunities to teach people through the thousands of interactions they have, large and small.

Amplifiers create a learning environment in the relentless pursuit of improving the company and their colleagues. This drives a culture of excellence mindset. Amplifiers don't get hung up on achieving perfection, but they never settle for mediocrity. They pursue being better at each turn. By constantly trying to be better themselves and to better those around them, the sum total of their effort produces substantially better results.

The Amplifier Cell and the Power of Three

Companies are organized in a variety of ways. Typically, most companies have a relatively set top-down organizational chart. Some companies also mix in cross-functional, matrix, or team structures within their organization. Regardless of the official organizational structure, successful companies must understand the strengths and weaknesses of team performance and leadership capability across a wide spectrum of leadership attributes. Companies invest in uncovering and discovering these leadership attributes among their employees. However, they fail to assess and develop followership capabilities. Without this, they cannot truly discover the Amplifiers among their ranks.

Most work gets done through teams. One of the biggest mistakes that leaders make is that they assign the same key employees, who are usually Amplifiers, to many of their strategic initiatives. This common mistake happens because leaders often trust these Amplifiers and recognize how they will make a positive impact on their assigned initiatives. The problem is twofold. First, these Amplifiers get stretched too thin. When they are tasked with working on multiple strategic initiatives concurrently, they cannot effectively accomplish all the tasks necessary without the risk of burnout. The second issue is more important: because the leader has not effectively developed a wide enough network to identify and assess the Amplifiers in their organization, the pool of talent for consideration is not broad enough. This risk is further magnified by the fact that leaders themselves may operate in an echo chamber of similarly like-minded followers. Organizations that do a good job of identifying and developing followers have a deeper bench of talent to deploy on strategic initiatives.

Successful companies have figured out how to inject key talent and high-profile or critical roles throughout the organization. When done effectively, these key individuals can have an outsized effect on the teams with which they interact. This occurs because their influence over others has the power to raise their performance along with the performance of the team.

Many companies get work done through teams. How they assemble these teams is critical to their success. They may select individuals with certain domain expertise, access to information, or seniority. But successful teams have Amplifiers among them. Amplifiers are contagious. Their presence on a team unleashes greater followership among their colleagues.

One of the negative consequences of assigning top performers to lead teams is that others in the organization may aspire to be assigned to these high-profile teams in order to satisfy a need for perceived status. When employees desire to be part of a high-profile team to elevate their own prestige, the objective of the team loses its power.

Another consideration when creating high-impact teams for a particular initiative or transformational effort is the conscious decision to assign a diverse set of team members. The power of three is a key element in creating diversity within a team and enabling all voices and perspectives to be heard. There is a multiplier effect at play within any department or team. There exists both positive and negative influences on any team. The strongest companies have a powerful organizational culture filled with more Amplifiers and pragmatic followers. They have the power to extract negative influences like how the human body attacks a bad cell. However, organizations that have not done a good job nurturing a strong and aligned culture toward the common mission and goals have a harder time squashing the negative influences. In these organizations, negative thinking can take root and grow.

Amplifiers have a way of stepping in and helping their struggling team members accomplish their tasks. They realize that the strength of the team is only as strong as the weakest link. It is through their own enlightened self-interest and the interest of the common good that they willingly reach out and support their struggling colleagues.

One of the common traps that prevents companies from achieving at their top performance levels is departmental or functional fiefdoms. Throughout my years of working with companies of all sizes and across many industries, I have seen the corrosive infighting that happens between departments or teams. Employees within their group defend their turf or position while casting blame at other functions. Although it is a common human tendency to protect or control their functional domain, that possessive instinct is detrimental to the company's ability to achieve its overall mission or goals. Amplifiers have a tendency to see the big picture and help break down barriers caused by the fiefdom syndrome. Although difficult to do, the rewards achieved by these Amplifiers pay dividends by advancing corporate strategy and business outcomes.

In the traditional hierarchical organization, an employee may work for an effective leader. But due to the nature of cross-functional teams, that same employee may also work for a boss in a different part of the corporate hierarchy. This presents special challenges. If an organization fails to recognize and support followership throughout, the follower who pushes back on the leader may be encouraged by that leader. However, when the Amplifier pushes back on the boss, they may be discouraged by that boss. One of the strengthening elements of a strong culture is the ability for colleagues to challenge each other.

Amplifiers' Impact on Changing Work Patterns

Effective leadership and management in the twenty-first century continue to evolve and incorporate new methods and approaches for effectively organizing and accomplishing work for organizations. The major revolutions in management science are (1) the introduction of the gig economy, along with the side hustle, (2) the emergence of technology and the speed at which technology changes the manner in which work gets done, (3) the philosophy of workers' careers and their expectation for how long they will stay at a company, and (4) the widespread transition to remote working brought on by the global COVID-19 pandemic.

The twenty-first-century leaders need not only to manage the departments or functions effectively but also to incorporate these changes into their management style. The job of being an effective manager continues to grow and evolve over time. As the science of management matures, the management systems and tools become incorporated into commonplace methods, often during course curriculum or on-the-job training. Managers can then focus on newer methods and approaches to effectively manage their work groups. This is evident in management accounting, total quality management, supply chain management, and many other disciplines. Professionals entering into these fields generally have had exposure to these management methods as practitioners, and their managers can rely on a higher level of base knowledge.

Let's first look at what historically has been viewed as effective management and has been battle tested through management development and training programs, university curriculum, and executive training on management. Although the methods differ, fundamentally there are a few situations when Amplifiers can magnify the power of teams and support traditional management:

1. **Line supervision and management.** Line supervision involves managing the work and overseeing highly repetitive tasks to ensure that the work is completed in an effective manner. This includes work being completed by millions of workers on assembly lines, retail, construction, and other frontline workers. The work being performed in these functions typically requires a narrow range of skill to complete. The nature of this work would be considered routine. In this group of unskilled

workers, it is critical that the tasks be well defined so as to be repeatable and predictable. As the workers are performing these tasks, their output needs to be monitored and reviewed.

Within this category of management, we also consider the management and oversight of skilled workers, craftspeople, and others that possess certain capabilities necessary for completion of work. Despite having particular skills, they would not be considered knowledge workers. This can't be confused with skill because many of these workers are highly skilled. But there is a difference when making the necessary decisions to manage skilled workers than when supervising unskilled workers.

The relationship between leadership and management in the context of line management is important but not as critical as it is in other contexts. To manage unskilled or skilled labor effectively, supervisors and managers can rely more on command-and-control techniques. Because there is a narrowly defined set of outcomes, leadership per se is less critical than clear direction and oversight.

As previously mentioned, Amplifiers exist at all levels of the organization, including in the rank-and-file line workers. Recall, the current CEO of Walmart began his career unloading trucks. We can imagine how he would have been helpful to his colleagues who were not destined to ascend the ranks of the company, but likely remain in positions closely related to the entry and lower-skilled levels. On the line, Amplifiers become the go-to people for their coworkers: they answer questions, pitch in to help in particular areas, and teach new hires coming on to the team. When the inevitable frustration with superiors boils up on the front line, Amplifiers have the credibility to relay the leader's rationale and fill in the communication gap, to essentially serve as their surrogate, and to be a change agent in the trenches. Amplifiers also have the courage to bring issues or better methods to achieve work outputs to their leaders or supervisors in a productive and action-oriented manner. This helps the company improve productivity and magnifies the power of teams.

2. **Management of knowledge workers.** Managing knowledge workers is far more challenging than managing the routine workers on the line. The category of knowledge workers is broad, and by definition, knowledge workers rely on their intellectual capability and critical thinking skills to accomplish their tasks. Knowledge workers can exist in organizations of any size, but certainly exist in virtually all medium- to large-scale enterprises.

   Over the years, we have seen many companies invest in the development of managers to enable them to be most effective in how they manage and oversee knowledge workers. The interplay between effective management and leadership for knowledge workers is critical. Although knowledge workers rely on their knowledge to complete their work, they equally rely on inspiration and influence from their manager leaders.

   Many line supervisors or managers are not well equipped to grow leaders or more effective followers. Amplifiers fill in this gap by role-modeling the behavior necessary and proactively coaching or mentoring their colleagues. This happens on formal and informal bases. Knowledge workers have a passion for learning and growing. This is the fuel for Amplifiers. They are energized by learning new skills and applying that knowledge to solve practical challenges or exploit new opportunities facing the company.

3. **Project and program management.** Project and program management differ in many regards from management of knowledge workers, as well as line supervision of skilled or unskilled labor. Generally speaking, managing projects or transformation efforts presents the manager with more challenges than overseeing a particular function. Most projects within a company incorporate various functions or disciplines and may use internal and external knowledge workers to complete the project.

   One of the key challenges of managing these interdisciplinary or cross-functional project teams is that many times the managers don't have actual control of the individuals who need to complete the work. In other cases, the work that is being done on the project will affect other groups or departments in the organization. As such, effective managers need to engage with the workers' direct supervisors and prioritize work across multiple functions.

Leadership becomes a critical part of an effective project or program manager's repertoire. In most cases, the manager needs to manage the work that needs to get done and also influence other stakeholders or their subordinates in order to accomplish the work and, more importantly, deliver the intended outcomes.

Most project and program management requires a high level of change necessary for the initiative to be successful. Amplifiers are change agents and they thrive on wielding their influence to enable their colleagues to willingly accept the new market, opportunity, or way of doing business. Amplifiers don't try to change minds directly or by force; they peddle influence, lead by example, or persuade others that the new way is worth pursuing. Because they have earned trust and credibility among their followers and other colleagues, Amplifiers can present a more compelling case on behalf of leaders because it is more grounded in the real-world, day-to-day life of the team on the ground that will be implementing the change.

4. **Enterprise or organizational management.** Enterprise or organizational management comes to life at the apex of the pyramids within an organization, ultimately to the top. These are functional, organizational, geographical, or other logical breakdowns of the management of a particular group within an organization.

Common tasks necessary to manage at this level include planning and forecasting, developing and organizing talent, problem-solving and issue resolution, and communications and reporting. We described previously in this book the differences between leadership and management. It is within this category of management where the differences between leadership and management are commonly misunderstood. Effective management typically has elements of leadership embedded in its operating style. However, we have seen countless managers who were ineffective leaders yet still were effective in managing the work group or function.

Amplifiers fill in the leadership gaps that inevitably exist in most companies. They bridge the gap between titled executives or bosses and the organization under their control. Amplifiers are motivated to produce results, and where a void exists, they seamlessly fill the gap and provide the leadership for the remainder of the team. At times, this is done consciously; other times, Amplifiers lead by example and others quickly latch on to their lead and follow them. Where there are strong leaders, Amplifiers enable these leaders to accomplish significantly more than they could ever accomplish alone. The leaders delegate authority to Amplifiers, and by doing so the leader is able to rest assured that the work will be handled while the leader can pick off other strategic priorities. This symbiotic relationship between leader and Amplifier creates a powerful impact on the aspects of the company they oversee.

5. **Self-management.** One of the most important elements of management, and it applies to everyone, is the management of ourselves. We think of management or supervisors as having the ability to manage others. However, if individuals lack the ability to manage their own activities or individual behaviors, they will not be able to effectively take on the management of others. Common elements of effective self-management are basic behaviors such as time management, delivering on commitments, taking pride in a job well done, effectively communicating, and the like.

The rise of the contingent workforce, independent contractors, and the gig economy demonstrates how self-managed individuals can, in fact, create rewarding careers by managing their own time and effort.

The best way for Amplifiers to influence the self-management of workers is for them to be a role model of the behavior necessary for success. Amplifiers do very well whether they are directly managed or if they work for a micromanager. Their strength lies not in their boss, but in their ability to adapt their styles to the situation. Amplifiers are self-motivated yet gain strength from other leaders and Amplifiers.

Challenges Facing Companies Today

Let's pivot to look at some of the management challenges presented in the twenty-first century. As younger workers enter the workforce, the social contract between employers and employees continues to evolve. The needs of these younger workers are creating different management challenges and are stretching some old management methods to new bounds.

The digital economy has created an environment where impressive careers can be created in a portable or easily transitory way. There is no longer the dependence on big companies with conventional career tracks to create sustainable professional growth. Although employers still look at job hoppers with skepticism when reviewing job candidates for positions, the amount of information and access to jobs generally favors the job seekers over employers.

Virtual Work and Managing Remote Work Groups

The global COVID-19 pandemic proved that knowledge workers can effectively get their work done in a remote fashion. A few months ago, I was reflecting with several fellow leaders on how difficult it would have been if the pandemic had hit in September 2001 rather than March 2020. When the terrorists struck on 9/11, the country essentially shut down for a week and then was crippled for months thereafter. The technology was not in place to effectively support remote work at scale. But 2020 proved to be a very different world from a technology perspective. We were grateful that these technological advancements enabled us to effectively keep employees on the payroll in a productive manner and at scale. This would have been nearly impossible twenty years ago. The damage to the economy would have been exponentially worse than it was.

Remote work is not new, nor is it a fad. Some companies have been leveraging some degree of remote work for decades. It has been interesting for me to see in conversations that I've had with executives some long-held notions that they need to "see the whites of the eyes" of the people performing the work in their offices. Global companies have become more comfortable with getting work done in remote offices, especially as many have offshored certain back office functions to lower-cost labor markets. But even these moves have generally been to offices or office settings of their business partners. For some companies and industries, working out of the travel bag and a briefcase regardless of where one's physical office is has always been a reality of the job. But when the pandemic hit, most companies were immediately thrust into a virtual working environment, at least for their white-collar workforce.

Company and employee reactions have varied widely. Some younger workers have moved back in with their parents. Others have taken their work out of densely populated cities and temporarily relocated to vacation homes, Airbnb's, or campers. The expectation that managers need to see their teams in person on a daily basis has been shattered. Some companies have made proclamations that they are "returning to normal" as soon as they can. Others are throwing in the towel on their lease obligations and vowing never to return to the office. We think that a third option consisting of a new normal that comprises office environments and virtual work will become the norm. Culture and team building are such a strong part of building a world-class company that the human element in interactions in real time with close proximity will be a critical part of ongoing culture building. Although the evidence is still being collected and it's too early to tell, one of the early signals from the leaders we know is their concern about the ability of their teams to effectively share knowledge, groom people, see and learn by example, and many of the other benefits derived from an office setting. Technology has improved significantly but we have not fully appreciated the technology corollary to the micro-interactions that are so crucial for career growth and strong culture building.

Typically, companies have some sort of matrix organization in which an employee may report functionally to one manager and also to another based on geography. But even in these circumstances, most managers at most organizations have been able to spend significant time with their direct reports or travel has enabled them to have frequent interactions. Managers have had to adjust how they manage their work groups. We are studying the impact of Amplifier behavior on the impact of virtual teams because we expect this to evolve as the workforce remains remote.

Impact of Technology Innovation on How Work Gets Done

Technology is changing the way work gets done at an exponential pace. Technology innovation is affecting how marketers acquire new customers, scientists develop new drugs, supply chains optimize inventory and delivery reliability, financial markets fund companies, and the list goes on. These technological changes affect the way knowledge workers complete their activities, but more important, they affect how effective managers must think about how their function will need to adapt in the future.

Early in my career, I worked for a major hotel company. The company was known in the industry as being one of the biggest and well-managed businesses. One of the interesting challenges well-run companies have is the ability to embrace new methods. Successful companies often fall into the trap of replicating their successful models at a larger scale. Great companies understand that good is the enemy of the best and that good companies need to innovate in order to do bigger things better in the future. The hotel chain would look at each development as an individual project, with an individual budget, and with individual oversight. Early in their evolution and their construction project division, small teams of buyers could easily see across the different projects they had underway and obtain purchasing synergies. But as they grew, they no longer were able to see and track prices they were paying for the exact or similar items for hotels they were building in different markets. Technology enabled them to standardize their master data and procurement planning. Thus, they were able to save hundreds of millions of dollars in the construction of new hotels. It seems like a simple example today, but at the time it was a revolutionary concept.

Digitally enabling customer and consumer behavior and activities have also changed the work that knowledge workers need to perform. Many companies have created digital platforms that enable self-service in the role of the customer service group, becoming more of a help desk or navigator for their customers to complete their tasks. Today, most seasoned travelers are annoyed if they have to stop by the front desk of the hotel before checking into their rooms. Hotel companies have leveraged technology to enable their guests to check in via a mobile device. This digital advancement is cost-effective for the hotel operator, as well as beneficial for their time-starved customers.

The global COVID-19 pandemic in triggered a number of urgent technology and digital changes to enable companies to get their goods or services into the hands of their consumers in a seamless way. The velocity of change brought about by technology is increasing and creating significant disruption to how effective managers oversee their work groups. Some companies, including one of the leading national banks, is requiring basic technology skills for all of their skilled workers. They believe that technology will play a vital role in any knowledge worker's position and that possessing technology skills is a necessary skill for employment. All of this has an impact on how companies should be thinking about their total talent strategies.

The Gig Economy and the Side Hustle

One of the changes the twenty-first century is bringing to the way work is being done is evident in the gig economy and the side hustle. Because technology has evolved to the point where knowledge workers can work from anywhere at any time, many are finding work beyond their primary employer whether it is inside or outside their primary field.

Managing gig economy workers is different than managing employees at your company. Different challenges exist for transient knowledge workers, such as ownership of the work product, disclosure, work standards and quality, and collaboration, which are critical for management. However, from a total talent perspective, having access to the gig economy, or micro-workers, can be an essential tool in the human capital tool bag.

With the emergence of the gig economy, many employees are actually performing work on the side at a larger scale. These side hustles are becoming a more common challenge for managers and leaders. Companies expect complete commitment of their full-time employees, yet a growing percentage of their workers produce income from their time serving others as well. This is common for designers, technology developers, accountants, and other positions that rely on their knowledge or advice and are further fueled by the ability to side hustle in a virtual setting.

Career Loyalty in the New Generation of Employees

As a new generation of workers enters the workforce, they are not looking for lifetime careers. Employers and managers have a growing challenge to make sure that the work environment and the work itself is rewarding and stimulating in order to retain top talent. With the onset of digital platforms for employees to easily find new jobs, there is more at stake and requires employers to pay greater attention to their employees. Because employees in this new generation have tempered expectations for lifelong careers with their employers, they are placing even more value in other aspects of their job, such as working for companies with a strong purpose, who are good corporate citizens, value diversity, equity, and inclusion, and offer work-life harmony.

6

Leadership Styles, Motives, and Traits

There are different styles, traits, and motives that are necessary for effective leadership, followership, and Amplifier behavior. It's also important to consider that these characteristics will likely change under varying conditions and should be applied situationally. For example, when a major shock rocks the economy, or a major societal movement gains momentum, leaders need to adjust their style to fit the situation and outside forces confronting the organization. There has been a great deal of prior work on leadership theory, including traits and styles. We added to the research to incorporate motives. Further we included our study of followers and Amplifiers into this analysis.

Leadership Styles

There is a large and established body of work on leadership styles and why leaders should understand their leadership style. Unfortunately, because there is such widespread misunderstanding of what true leadership really is, these styles don't always hit the mark. Leadership is different than management. As a result, our premise on leadership is not based solely on who happens to be in the top spot or position overseeing others. Titled executives are in charge, for sure, but that does not mean leadership. We also look at the sustainability of leadership. The transient leader may garner followers in the short term, but these followers will eventually become disillusioned and fade away as the shallowness of the transient leader's substance is revealed.

Our analysis in Amplifiers takes a fresh look at these styles and strips out the styles that are more closely aligned with titled executives or bosses. We include them because they provide a useful contrast to true leadership and Amplifier styles. We recognize, however, that there are certain times when leaders need to use one of these titled executive styles. We identify these styles as management styles, not leadership or Amplifier styles. We evaluate leadership styles through the lens of the leaders-bosses axis and plot the styles along that continuum. In this analysis, we explore new styles that are better suited for true leaders and appropriately categorize executive orders as management tools, not leadership styles.

Table 6.1 summarizes the styles that we've commonly seen in research and various leadership development programs. We parse

Table 6.1   Styles in Leadership Development Programs

Common Leadership Style	Management/Leadership/ Amplifier Style
1. Authoritative or autocratic	Management
2. Charismatic	Leadership
3. Exemplary	Amplifier
4. Laissez-faire	Leadership/Amplifier
5. Level 5	Leadership/Amplifier
6. Motivational	Leadership
7. Participative or democratic	Management
8. Principled	Leadership/Amplifier
9. Servant	Leadership/Amplifier
10. Transactional	Management
11. Transformational	Leadership

them to highlight whether they are reflective of leadership versus management because some of the styles are indications of bosses not leaders. We also highlight those styles that are indicative of Amplifiers. Generally speaking, there is one or two dominant styles that most individuals display. We appreciate that in real-life situations, effective leaders and titled executives typically use any or all styles on a situational basis in order to drive the best possible outcome for the company.

Authoritative or Autocratic (Style: Management)

Authoritative executives rely on their power or position to make decisions and drive behavior. Typically, executives with this style like to make decisions themselves, with or without input from others. One could consider dictators to be autocratic leaders. The main benefit of this style is that decisions can be made quickly. The downside is that decisions may not be fully considered and not capture sufficient alternative or diverse points of view. This style expects decisions to cascade down throughout the organization, driven from the top. It works best in orderly and hierarchical organizations with strong deference to titles and power.

The autocrat does not foster a culture of dissent or debate in order to discover a better direction or strategy. They do not like being called out in public or in meetings if subordinates disagree with their point of view. Their attitude is very much "my way or the highway." They expect compliance and punish nonconformists.

Charismatic (Style: Leadership)

Charismatic leaders rely on frothy emotional appeals and rallies to deliver their message. Their speeches and presentations are eloquent and rely on persuasive rhetoric. These leaders are typically gregarious, outspoken, and the center of attention. They have a tendency to garner rock star status and oftentimes the company becomes more about the leader, rather than the leader acting as a servant to the company. Leaders of this type are very concerned about how they appear to others and how their message is received, more so than the depth of understanding of the audience. Charismatic leaders are often visible ambassadors in external media or even in their company's advertising campaigns.

Charismatic leaders don't sweat the details or spend much time managing tasks or activities to accomplish corporate goals. They rely on key followers to handle these activities. This leadership style is not a successful long-term style if it is not coupled with greater substance.

Exemplary (Style: Amplifier)

Some leaders lead by example. Generally speaking, all leaders lead by example to a certain degree. But in this context, when a leader creates a picture of what's possible and jumps in to turn the possibility into a reality, they inspire followers to approach the challenge with the attitude, "if they can do it, I can do it." Exemplary leaders make it safe and easy for followers to join. Exemplary leaders have a proven track record and subject matter knowledge that gives the organization confidence that the leader has walked in their shoes before and that what they're suggesting is possible. We have seen the opposite, when executives with no practical experience in a particular area direct others to do the dirty work. Followers sense when executives are asking them to do things they wouldn't, or can't, do themselves. When followers recognize that an executive has done it and would do it again time permitting, they will go to great lengths for that leader. The downside of exemplary leadership is that the hands-on nature may distract the executive from attending to other pressing needs.

Laissez-Faire (Style: Leadership/Amplifier)

Laissez-faire is a hands-off leadership style. This is a form of empowering leadership style in which leaders empower their teams by returning authority to their followers. The leader clearly communicates the strategic vision, goals, and expectations for excellence. With that foundation in place, the leader allows for followers to deliver results in accordance with the followers' own particular styles, objectives, and tactical plans. In stark contrast to micromanagers, these leaders resist the urge to get involved but are willing and able to step in to help should their followers need support. This type of strategy is common for leaders to grant to regional or geographic general managers or divisions within a multidivisional conglomerate. Warren Buffet's style is laissez-faire with respect to the independent operating companies within Berkshire Hathaway.

This style can't be confused with lack of caring because leaders with this style care deeply about the business performance and the followers who are leading the teams for them. One trap that leaders can make with this style is the temptation to get involved in decisions without being invited by their followers to do so. Leaders who have "been there, done that" and have a lot of expertise in an area need to remain at arm's length and let their teams make and learn from their own mistakes.

Level 5 (Style: Leadership/Amplifier)

The Level 5 leader is a concept created by Jim Collins in his book, *Good to Great*. Collins summarizes the Level 5 leaders as those who channel their ego needs away from themselves and into the larger goal of building a great company. It's not that Level 5 leaders lack an ego or self-interest. Indeed, they are incredibly ambitious—*but their ambition is first and foremost for the institution not themselves.*[1] These leaders possess the capabilities and responsibilities of an effective leader, but furthermore, they possess a sense of humility and professional will that sets them apart from other leaders.

Motivational (Style: Leadership)

Motivational leaders are often charismatic by nature and have a way of painting a picture or vision that energizes followers to act. These leaders are approachable and engaged, providing encouragement and support to their followers. The team sees the leader as being in the trenches, garnering their trust and respect. Motivational leaders are optimistic and will set high, yet achievable standards and push the team to accomplish the goals. Effective motivators are demanding but create a clear road map for followers to learn and grow, while providing the necessary resources to be successful.

Participative or Democratic (Style: Management)

Democratic executives rely on majority rule or quorums to arrive at decisions. They operate in a manner and style that shares decision-making with the group or team members in order to obtain their buy-in and commitment, as well as capturing a broad set of perspectives. These executives will run workshops, commission teams, or work streams and meet to sift through and synthesize a vast number of inputs to form a solid foundation for the decision. These team work group sessions capture input regardless of organizational role or hierarchy providing an equal basis to inform the decision. This style is the opposite of the autocratic style. It has a tendency for decisions to take longer to make because of the need to achieve broad-based buy-in. Yet when it works, commitment helps to achieve greater stickiness of the decisions in the organization.

Principled (Style: Leadership/Amplifier)

Principled leaders are guided by principles to make their decisions. These can be as simple as "customer first," "employee first," or "do the right thing." Leaders with a principled style have little tolerance when followers cut corners or violate the central principle or core value. They are culture builders and recruit new talent that is aligned with the company's principles.

Servant (Style: Leadership/Amplifier)

Servant leaders focus their time and energy on how they can serve their stakeholders because they believe that only by helping others will they, or their organizations, be successful. Servant leaders prioritize the needs of others over their own. Creating a strong culture is an essential element for servant leadership to be effective. Many companies with a clear higher purpose, such as curing cancer, are good candidates for servant leaders to be spread throughout the rank-and-file organization. Followers tend to place a high level of trust in servant leaders because they recognize that these leaders are subordinating their own self-interest on behalf of the organization's greater purpose.

Transactional (Style: Management)

Transactional executives are driven by the philosophy of the carrot and the stick. Subordinates will perform tasks assigned to them by the executive, who will in turn reward or reprimand the subordinate based on their achievement or lack thereof—many times in public to set an example. Subordinates come to rely on or fear such praise and punishments; they tend to focus on the executive's anticipated response rather than optimally performing the task at hand. This style works best in hierarchical or bureaucratic organizational structures because it is highly directive. Although the style provides clear direction, it limits the creativity and innovation available to the company.

Transformational (Style: Leadership)

Transformational leaders are change-oriented executives with a future vision for the organization beyond its current capabilities or product/service mix. They have high expectations and aspirations, and they are constantly pushing the company to achieve new levels of performance. Status quo is the arch enemy of transformational leaders. Transformational leaders tend to empower teams, are more entrepreneurial, and push for innovation. They believe that if the organization is not evolving, it will not keep pace with the competitive market. They are not afraid to cannibalize their current product portfolio in order to remain relevant for the future.

Leadership Motives

True leaders are motivated to act for a variety of reasons. Throughout our experience working with companies, we have seen profiles of executives who have had different motives that influence their leadership style. There has been very little external research on the topic, and our observations are in fact nascent.

Motives matter a lot. Yet they are often not well known among employees, customers, shareholders, and other stakeholders. A motive is defined as a reason for doing something, especially one that is *hidden or not obvious*. Motives can be good or bad. They can be self-serving or altruistic. Every leader and titled executive has their own motives, and they should be scrutinized for their seen and unseen actions. The understanding of motives at the top is a leading indicator for how decisions will be made, the leadership style deployed, the treatment of constituents, and alignment with the future success of the enterprise.

The most important role a board of directors has is the hiring and firing of the CEO. Therefore, they need to understand the CEO's motives and motivations. Alignment of the board's motives and the CEO's motives are critical to ensure that the right person is in the top spot. However, there are leaders and managers throughout a company, and motives at every level are crucial to ensure alignment of behavior and drive corporate performance. The following motives are the most common that we have seen demonstrated among the leaders and executives we studied.

Drive and Achievement

Some leaders are motivated by drive and accomplishment. These are highly competitive leaders with a long history of personal achievements. The relentless pursuit of achieving the goals set forth before them, their ability to execute, and leadership skills propelled them up the proverbial ladder as increasing levels of responsibility were bestowed on them. These leaders are driven by their ability to compete and win. At its core, it is a self-oriented motive.

Higher Purpose

Pursuing a higher purpose is a key motive for some leaders and executives. In fact, some companies have built an entire franchise on achieving an aspect of the greater good. This can be as lofty as to cure cancer (Celgene), to improve access to healthy food options for consumers (Whole Foods), or to enable any American the convenience of transportation (the early days of Ford Motor Company).

Legacy

Creating a legacy for either the leader or the company is another motive that drives behavior. Legacy-focused leaders take a very long view of the organizations under their care. We see leaders developed or appointed at companies with a high degree of family ownership, like Brown-Forman, Estee Lauder, Ford, Walmart, and others. When a family name is on the company letterhead, there is usually a much longer decision time frame—and are far less interested in short-term quarterly earnings. We have noticed that some of the best run boards have this family dynamic in the shareholder base. We also see this motive in founder-led firms such as Amazon, Microsoft (under Gates), Apple (under Jobs), and Tesla. Legacy-oriented leaders are typically altruistic. Although they tend to benefit personally, this is a byproduct of their contributions, not the result of their pursuit for rewards.

Power

Some executives are motivated by power. Power is a potent drug for rising executives. As they are exposed to power and influence, they crave more. This leadership motive is more prevalent in old-line companies that are well established. When unchecked, it produces bad results because the executive is far more focused on rising in position than in actual achievement of the organization's strategic goals. The formality, pomp, and circumstance surrounding power-hungry executives becomes their driving force and fuel. The rise and fall of Jeff Immelt is an example of a power-oriented executive developed in a culture that placed a premium on position power over substance.

Preservation

There are executives who are content with preserving the core strengths of the company and not rocking the boat under their watch. We see this in many companies that largely track the consumer price index and have very stable customer and competitive forces. Some cash cow companies in dying markets also pursue a preservation strategy to milk the cash flow of the remaining life of the product line. Leaders with this motive typically make incremental changes and value conformance over innovation. They want to leave the organization to the next leader in as good or a better position.

Rewards and Recognition

Executives motivated by rewards or recognition are easy to spot. The advantage to this motive is that it is easy to align the corporate goals with the compensation/reward plan for the executive. Always on the search for a pat on the back, these executives have a high self-orientation and often place their own personal fame ahead of the company's reputation. In addition, executives with this motive will try to renegotiate their pay packages when the external environment changes. We also see these executives feel internal pressure to hit quarterly numbers, which if unchecked, may drive questionable decisions.

Leadership Traits

1. **Accountable.** Accountability is a critical quality for effective leadership. Being accountable requires leaders to put themselves out in front of their constituents to explain results or actions the organization has taken. The best leaders usually share the credit and bear the criticism. Leaders take responsibility for mistakes. There are always outside factors that may affect the particular strategy or course of action, and leaders may explain these factors for context, but they will not blame outside factors for the results under their command. There is nothing more unflattering and pathetic than individuals holding the microphone and

blaming others for poor performance or mistakes made under their watch. Accountability goes hand in hand with integrity and earns respect.

2. **Amplifier.** An Amplifier is a leader who displays strong leadership and followership capabilities that are combined in a uniquely synthesized manner to increase the power of leadership. Amplifiers take the power of the signal, whether it be strategy, initiatives, culture, and so on, enlarge it, and magnify it out to the broader organization.

3. **Astute.** The best leaders are astutely aware of their surroundings. This perception occurs in a physical and emotional sense. The best leaders are able to process information that is presented to them on paper, as well as sense the environmental context their decision will affect. They have a keen sense of what's moving the markets and resulting actions the company should take. They understand cultural shifts occurring in the firm and use this to advocate change. We have often heard that the best leaders "trust their gut." This instinct comes from their astute connection to their surroundings, historical facts, trends, and the talent required to execute within that context.

4. **Charismatic.** The charismatic leader motivates followers in confident and flashy speeches, often with a high degree of fanfare and with particular eloquence. However, it is often the Potemkin village of leadership. Followers fall prey to the façade of leadership through charisma when there is no actual leadership substance beneath the surface. This quality is most visible and least valuable. Unfortunately for these transient leaders and their followers, there needs to exist substance underneath the charismatic surface. Most followers require substance from their leaders. In order for leadership to transcend the inevitable peaks and valleys in the difficult times, the leaders need to make substantive contributions or their followers will fall away.

5. **Committed.** Leaders are committed to the cause or mission of the organization. Over the years working with organizations

of all sizes, we've seen large projects that have consumed vast resources yet failed to have the executive commitment necessary for success. Followers within an organization easily sense when a leader is not committed to a particular strategy, project, or proclamation. On the flip side, when followers sense that leaders are committed to pursuing a particular course of action, and they are diving headfirst into the pursuit, employees will follow the leader into the initiative.

6. **Communicator.** Effective leaders are good communicators. The best communication is timely, direct, straightforward, sincere, and concise. Followers want to know who, what, when, why, and how. To be sure, good communication is not measured in volume. Some leaders have a way of delivering ten minutes of content in an hour talk. This is lazy and disrespectful to the audience. Mark Twain is known to have said, "If I had more time, I would have written a shorter letter." One of the most popular orators of his time, Edward Everett gave a two-hour speech in Gettysburg that nobody remembers. Abraham Lincoln delivered the Gettysburg address, all 272 words of it, in two minutes. It was one of the most powerful speeches ever given. The speech itself is filled with leadership lessons of humility, grace, commitment, and higher purpose.

7. **Confident.** Confidence is contagious—people want to see confidence in the people they follow. When leaders lead confidently, the followers share that confidence. However, like charisma, confidence is a precarious leadership trait. Too much confidence actually becomes a liability. There is a yin and a yang regarding the interplay ego has with confidence. Overconfident or egotistical leaders may garner followers for a short period of time, but it's usually not sustainable. On the flip side, the buck stops with the leaders, and they need to have the confidence in the decisions they're making. Leaders must have a strong enough ego to withstand the inevitable skeptics and critics of their particular strategy or vision.

8. **Courageous.** Being courageous is essential for effective leadership. Leaders need to be willing to take the right course of action regardless of popularity or consensus and regardless of personal or professional risk. Human nature is driven by all kinds of fear. Most fear is driven by something someone feels they will lose or not achieve. Courage is the antidote to fear. Knowing that fear drives all sorts of perverse human behavior, people need to see courage among their leaders. Many decisions are made by myriad leaders peppered throughout the organization. Not all of these decisions are easy to make. The leaders faced with making a tough decision have the voices in their heads casting fear, uncertainty, and doubt. "Do I have all the information? If I make the wrong call, will I lose my job?" And the list goes on. There are also some decisions that can only be made at the top. Although there is a saying, "it's lonely at the top," the best leaders are also Amplifiers and, as such, solicit input from their trusted critics. Nonetheless, leaders need to make the decisions that only they can make. This requires courage.

   Incorporating the appropriate level of risk tolerance is another derivative of courage. There are many times that leaders have to make a decision without all the information available. Leaders constantly need to balance risk and reward across a whole host of measures. Effective leaders need to sift through the information at their disposal, weigh the risks, and make a decision. Having tolerance for risk does not mean that leaders can cross an ethical line; it means that they recognize the outcomes are not sure bets and that decisions they make may not turn out well.

9. **Credible.** Leaders ascend into positions of power for a variety of reasons. Generally, they don't last long if they don't have credibility with their followers. Credibility is gained through experience, education, or input from other close trusted advisors. Competence is a prerequisite for credibility. Leaders also gain credibility when they admit they don't know something

and rely on a colleague to supply the knowledge or information missing. It's unreasonable to expect that leaders know everything. But it's fully within reason to expect leaders to learn and demonstrate competence in their particular area, markets, or domain.

10. **Decisive.** In order for organizations to make progress, leaders must make countless decisions every day: some mundane, but more likely complex. In some circumstances, there is sufficient information available for a quick decision to be made. In other cases, especially those involving new or complex issues, additional information may be required. Occasionally, time constraints or other factors will render a complete fact base impossible prior to a decision being necessary. Leaders need to assess the information at their disposal, risks associated, and other impacts, and make a decision in a timely fashion. We have all seen people, even at senior roles within a company, waffle and drag out decisions for an extended time. Indecisiveness and waffling are the death knell of many strategy or transformation efforts.

11. **Empowering.** Every great leader knows they cannot make all of the decisions necessary to carry out the daily activities of any organization. Great leaders empower their followers to act. Leaders grant responsibility and accountability to their teams, especially as they progress in roles with increasing responsibility. Some leaders call this "returning authority" to their teams. When leaders return authority to their subordinates, they must trust their followers to make the decisions. For some leaders, this is extremely difficult because they have very strong opinions about the end result or how the decision should be made. Leaders must let those followers learn from the mistakes they will inevitably make along the journey. When a follower is responsible for making a decision and brings it forward, the leader has a responsibility to guide the decision-making but not to make the decision for them. Another trap leaders face is that they are typically very capable performing the tasks or

activities themselves. But they cannot effectively leverage all the resources and talents within the company if they are doing the work that others can aptly do. Because they can doesn't mean they should. In fact, this would be a significant disservice to the development of their followers. Great leaders find ways to empower others to get the work done by making appropriate decisions and offering constructive guidance.

12. **Entrepreneurial.** We define the entrepreneurial leadership trait as the ability to identify an unmet need or opportunity, the willingness to assume risk, the courage to fail, and the conviction to see an idea through. We expect leaders to have skin in the game as they progress their ideas forward. Being entrepreneurial does not mean that everyone needs to go out and start their own company. But they do need to have a vested stake in the ideas they propose and the willingness to stick their neck out while engaging in the pursuit of a new venture, product/service, market, or process improvement.

13. **Fair/Just.** Followers will follow leaders when they see that they will be treated fairly and with respect. They expect justice when unfair practices or behaviors are demonstrated by their colleagues at the company. One of the traps leaders fall into is that they have a tendency to pick the same high-performing followers for the high-profile and plum assignments. Although they do this with the intention of delivering the best possible result for the company, they fail to understand that by relying on a small few for key assignments, the organization does not fully tap the cadre of talent at their disposal. It is far more effective to tap a broader set of employees to work on strategic initiatives to increase diversity of thought, perspectives, and minimize echo chambers.

14. **Followership.** With the rare exception of co-CEOs, there is only one person at the top. However, most organizations are filled with hundreds or thousands of other leaders who report to other leaders or bosses. This means that there are exponentially more followers in the best run companies than there are

leaders because great followers are also leaders themselves. Followership is not the opposite of leadership. It is a different dimension entirely.

The best followers are critical and independent thinkers who take an active role in advancing corporate strategy and culture for the good of all the stakeholders. They are not sheep blindly following a leader. They are lifelong learners and teachers constantly in pursuit of creating better outcomes for all. We define followership as those who possess the attributes of positive, active, and independent thinkers, who evaluate actions or decisions as opposed to blindly accepting them; they voice differences in a constructive manner and ultimately support the group's decisions as if they were their own.

15. **Humble**. Jim Collins popularized humility as a leadership trait in his book *Good to Great*. He discusses the Level 5 leader as having a unique combination of personal humility and professional will. Humility didn't seem to be a positive character trait for me as an arrogant youth growing up. However, as I look back over my career, every single great leader whom I encountered had a healthy dose of humility. These leaders did not let arrogance trip them up. Followers respect when leaders admit mistakes. You need humility to admit your mistakes. Followers also gain confidence when they feel that the leaders have a true sense of what the organization can accomplish, and it's not built on sand or puffed up by rosy projections. The other element of humility is that great leaders don't need to stand up and take credit for the successes of the company. They usually are the first to give credit generously while accepting all criticism.

16. **Inclusive**. Great leaders fully appreciate the diverse set of experiences and voices that can help create an even better organization. They understand the importance of investing in a more diverse, equitable, and inclusive organization. Over the years, I've met numerous executive teams, steering committees, boards, and so on that have not been inclusive. Most of our global clients have been around for decades, and inclusivity

requires an evolution from older thinking. The best companies are inserting leaders with inclusive styles who are committed to changing the composition of the companies they shepherd to better reflect the thoughts and ideas of the populations they serve. Great leaders ensure that all their employees have a consistent and equitable career experience with equal access to opportunities and resources to enhance their careers.

17. **Inspirational.** Great leaders inspire followers to pursue a particular mission or strategy. They have a way of connecting by understanding the needs of the followers in order to create a vision that inspires followers to take action. The style of delivery is less important than the inspirational message the leader delivers. Inspirational leaders are able to tap the hearts and minds of their followers to compel them to act.

18. **Integrity.** Integrity seems like a logical no-brainer character trait for leaders. But it's surprising how many titled executives are promoted without fully evolving this trait. Organizations expect their leaders to adhere to a set of moral and ethical principles. Unfortunately, there are far too many organizations that have gone astray from morals and principles, such as Volkswagen, Boeing, Wells Fargo, Enron, Tyco, and the list goes on. In all of these cases, there was a lack of integrity at the top that transcended to the culture and behaviors of the organization.

    Another manifestation of integrity is the level of transparency leaders communicate throughout the organization. This doesn't mean that leaders should tell everyone everything, but what they communicate should be truthful and complete based on the knowledge they have. Information flows at a dramatically increased speed today more than it ever has in the past. When leaders inflate forecasts or projections that are not based in fact, they lose credibility by compromising their integrity in their communications.

19. **Loyal.** Great leaders have a tendency to be very loyal, not just to the organization but also to their followers. This loyalty is generally a result of the mutual interactions they've had over

the years where the followers have helped the leaders ascend in their careers. For the most part, this loyalty is positive in that it is based on trust, credibility, familiarity, and a sense of mutual commitment. It breaks down, however, when the leader continuously favors those loyal followers because this can prevent an inclusive environment. Furthermore, it can be especially challenging when the leader needs to take a tough action against a loyal follower. Dealing with nonperforming loyal followers can be a difficult challenge for most leaders.

20. **Motivational.** One of the critical tasks required of leaders is to motivate their followers. This is especially true when the task at hand is very difficult or seemingly impossible. Motivational leaders have the ability to get others to perform at their best by building them up and giving them the confidence to believe in themselves and their ability to deliver on the mission. Effective leaders intuitively know how different individuals are motivated because not everyone is motivated the same way. Athletes know that when it's time to review film after the game they are going to get called out for all their mistakes in front of their teammates. When you blow an assignment, you should expect to get direct feedback, aggressively, in real time. Years ago, I put up a scorecard ranking A–F the performance of executives based on the key dimensions of performance. It did not go over well. It was this unfortunate leadership mistake when I realized that not everybody is motivated in the same way. My thinking along these lines has evolved to incorporate concepts from other examples. One such idea is to convert the ideas contained in *The Five Love Languages* by Gary Chapman into a professional setting. Some professionals are motivated by recognition (words of affection), others are motivated by monetary rewards (gifts), and yet others are motivated by the mission or purpose of the company (acts of service).[2]

21. **Optimistic.** Years ago, two of my partners gave a presentation to a large audience about leadership lessons learned from Winnie-the-Pooh's Hundred Acre Wood created by author A. A. Milne.[3]

In their presentation, they juxtaposed Tigger's eternal optimism with that of the ever-glum, sarcastic, and pessimistic Eeyore, noting that organizations need optimistic leaders to motivate their troops. Followers are not attracted to pessimism and sarcasm. They are attracted to optimistic leaders grounded in a realistic vision for a better future.

22. **Passionate.** Great leaders typically work long and hard at their jobs and often carry the burden of what they do home at night. For them to progress in their careers and obtain increasing responsibility and leadership, they need to be passionate about what they do. Any half-hearted attempt from a leader to cajole their followers into completing a task or assignment will not be effective. When leaders are passionate about the purpose and the course ahead to get there, their passion becomes infectious and others catch on.

23. **Presence and demeanor.** Presence and demeanor are important leadership traits. We think of it as the desire to engage and influence others while presenting oneself in a professional manner and remaining personally engaged, objective, and balanced. When leaders fly off the handle, they run the risk of their followers losing confidence in them. Highly emotional appeals often don't carry the day. Leaders need to be effective communicators and remain calm during difficult or tumultuous situations. Great leaders also have the ability to blend in and not always command the spotlight. They know when to sit back and observe while a situation unfolds, or when to step up and weigh in on a discussion. Often we witness great leaders speaking last, because they don't want their voice or opinion to either intimidate or stifle free thinking in the team. On the flip side, they know when to speak first to set the tone and clear direction for the team to follow.

24. **Reliable.** Effective leaders are reliable. As discussed previously, trust equals (credibility + reliability + intimacy) divided by self-orientation.[4] If followers can't count on an unreliable leader, they will lose respect for that individual. Leaders do what they

say they're going to do, and they expect others to do the same. Leaders can be depended on across a variety of dimensions to support followers.

25. **Selfless**. One of the most important leadership traits is selflessness. Selflessness is more than just being unselfish. Great leaders will go to extraordinary lengths for others. Over the years, I've encountered scores of executives who have had a high sense of self-worth and self-orientation. In virtually all cases, they do not create a lasting base of followers. Followers are attracted to leaders whom they know have subordinated their own self-interest to a higher purpose, the organization, or the followers themselves. There have been a number of studies that analyze the transcripts of earnings calls by CEOs in their use of the pronouns. Self-oriented CEOs tend to use self-inclusive language, like *I* or *me* when delivering good news and collective language, like *we* or *our* when delivering negative news, to which the market response has been negative.[5] Whereas it is an obvious indication of self-orientation, actions always speak louder than words.

26. **Studied**. Leaders are studied. As they are ascending in their career, most leaders don't appreciate that they are being watched and studied by their colleagues. People study them because they want to know what the organization values that's leading to their promotions. People study them in formal and informal ways. Being studied is a responsibility that some leaders fail to realize until it's too late. Followers study good habits as well as bad habits.

27. **Versatile**. Versatility is a trait that demonstrates leaders' ability to alter their leadership style to fit the needs of an individual or situation. Not all followers receive information the same way. Compounding this, not all followers react to a similar message in the same way. In order for leaders to get the most out of their teams, they may need to adapt their style to the teams they are trying to motivate or influence. It's critical that the versatility remains authentic, but the leadership tools

required for a particular group of people or in a particular situation can vary.

28. **Visionary.** One of the greatest responsibilities for any leader is to set the vision and strategy for the company. There is an element of creativity and aspiration needed to articulate an effective view of the enterprise's destination. Followers want to tap into the dream of the leader. Equally important, followers want to understand that despite lofty dreams, the leader's feet are firmly planted on the ground.

7

Followership Styles, Motives, and Traits

Effective followership is defined by a set of styles that followers display in order to accomplish the needs of the leader as well as provide leadership direction to their followers.

Followership Styles

A follower style is one that the follower uses to carry out the direction of the leader, fill the leadership void of a titled executive, and influence other followers to perform the work necessary to accomplish the goals set forth by the company. Different situations call for different followership styles. The style adopted should be one that best incorporates the strengths and weaknesses of the leader, the organization's objectives, and the professional and personal needs of the other followers.

Followers exist at all levels of the company. Tapping into the best followers to unleash the power of followership is an underappreciated tool available to companies. The range of follower activity spans from being a subordinate, order taker, or rule follower and blindly performing the tasks assigned at the one extreme. The other extreme, being an exemplary follower, requires active, innovative, and critical thinking, combined with a positive attitude, subject matter expertise (peer credibility), dedication to the leader's purpose and

Table 7.1   Followership Styles

Common Followership Style Descriptions	Subordinate/Followership/Amplifier Style
1. Compliant	Subordinate
2. Consigliere	Followership/Amplifier
3. Exemplary	Followership/Amplifier
4. Enabler	Followership
5. Position player	Subordinate
6. Trusted skeptic	Followership/Amplifier
7. Survivor	Subordinate

the organization's mission, and ability to get work done regardless of cultural barriers.

Table 7.1 highlights the common followership styles used by subordinates through effective followers as they progress in their careers. We juxtapose followership styles in a similar fashion to leadership styles across the spectrum and highlight them here for reference.

Compliant (Style: Subordinate)

Compliant followers are those individuals who are perfectly capable workers. They follow rules and directions from their superiors or leaders. These followers will carry out the orders from above in a reliable manner, but they will not engage in much critical thinking or put the task into the context of the bigger picture. Depending on their role within the organization, these subordinates can be essential. For example, many frontline positions on the production line, in a warehouse function, or in other lower skilled positions require individuals who are capable of doing their jobs in a reliable and repeatable fashion. Many future CEOs started out like this: as mentioned, Doug McMillon, the CEO of Walmart, began his career by unloading trucks. Undoubtedly, he was initially a compliant subordinate, although underneath he possessed many good leadership and followership traits.

Consigliere (Style: Followership/Amplifier)

The term *consigliere* originates from the Italian meaning "advisor or counselor." Although it is still a common title for members of city council in Italy, it has been popularized in English through writings about the mob. There are a few key aspects of the role of the consigliere. The first role is to be the primary and private trusted advisor to the leader. The consigliere has information and a special connection with the broader organization and brings that perspective to the leader to help shape key decisions that may have an impact for all stakeholders. In this capacity, the consigliere serves as a sounding board for the leader prior to key decisions being made. Another key element to the role is to represent the leader when the leader is not available. Other team members recognize that the consigliere can speak on behalf of the leader so that many times, team members will bring key decisions to the consigliere, either to get preliminary feedback on decisions or ideas or to seek approval to go forward in a particular direction. The consigliere holds a great deal of influence in the organization so long as their intent and motives closely aligns with that of the leader.

Exemplary (Style: Followership/Amplifier)

Exemplary followers demonstrate a high degree of independence and are the go-to professionals for a wide array of issues that arise during the normal course of operations. This followership style originated out of Robert Kelley's book the *Power of Followership*. Followers with this trait provide intelligent and sensitive support coupled with a challenging independent, innovative, and critical mindset in order to influence the leader and the team to arrive at a better decision or approach.[1] Exemplary followers are highly capable and possess subject matter expertise and competence in their field. They are able to blend this knowledge along with active participation and critical thinking to raise the bar for the entire team. They are oftentimes studied and emulated by other followers.

Enabler (Style: Followership)

The enabler is the kind of follower that makes things happen for the leader. They enable the leader to succeed and they take pride in doing so. Enablers are very competent in their jobs and possess deep subject matter expertise. However, they do not have the desire or ability to take on the pressure, responsibility, or accountability that rests on the leader's shoulders. Their personalities are better suited to being a supporting team member as opposed to being the person in charge of making the decisions or setting the direction for the organization. Highly competent and resourceful, enablers play a critical role in the leader's ability to get stuff done. But the leader needs to understand the limitations of the enabler because they lack elements of the exemplary follower.

Position Player (Style: Subordinate)

Every great organization has a significant number of employees who are solid position players. They clearly understand their job responsibilities and duties, carry them out in a professional and competent manner, and are willing to step in and help when called on. Position players take pride in the roles they serve, and they always want to perform better in those roles. Position players do not aspire to fill other leadership or related assignments; they garner substantial satisfaction by being recognized as highly competent in their current roles. These professionals are generally politically astute and, in some cases, have served in their positions for decades. They have broken in new managers or leaders above them and have helped train new colleagues as peers. It is this style that causes many change management initiatives to break down. Too often, leaders have failed to understand the role position players have during transformation efforts.

Trusted Skeptic (Style: Followership/Amplifier)

The trusted skeptic is a particularly important followership style. To be effective with this style, these followers need the trust and confidence of their leaders, combined with a high degree of personal expertise. They subordinate their own personal self-interest to the interest of the organization and the leader. They also have a significant foundation of knowledge of the issue at hand. From this vantage point, they can provide a healthy dose of honest criticism or skepticism about the direction or decisions the leaders may be contemplating. Because the trusted skeptic is, informed and has a convincing desire to improve the organization, the leader appreciates that the criticism is not personal and comes from a good and knowledgeable place.

Survivor (Style: Subordinate)

A survivor is a mediocre or incremental performer who is adept at navigating the politics of the organization. They are typically in their roles or positions for long periods of time before advancing to the next level, and many times they maintain their jobs long after their value has been exhausted. Large and established companies are filled with survivors. They are driven by the desire not to rock the boat for fear of reprisal or even losing their job. They make safe decisions and do not stick their necks out on the line. Generally speaking, they have a high degree of self-orientation and ask the question, "What's in it for me." These followers are at risk of being influenced by leaders with bad intent. As a result, because these followers comprise the critical population within the organization, leaders need to ensure they are aligned with the strategic direction and change in order for any major transformation initiative to take hold.

Followership Motives

Understanding the motives behind why some employees are supportive followers while other subordinates simply show up to work is a key insight needed to optimize corporate performance. Most organizations focus their time and energy on leadership development and in doing so miss an opportunity to develop the vast majority of the employee base. Diving into leadership development programs and styles is helpful. But understanding the motives behind why leaders lead and why followers follow is the difference between mediocrity in a company's culture and ultimately business performance.

We identify leadership styles, motives, and traits in chapter 6. Just as leadership/management motives range from effective leaders to titled bosses, the same range of motives applies to followers along their continuum. Followers range from subordinates through exemplary followers and have differing motives that drive their behavior depending on where they exist along the spectrum. Understanding the different motives of followers enables leaders to properly activate them to carry out corporate strategy execution or strategic initiatives.

Behind-the-Scenes Achiever

Behind every great leader, there is (at least) a great follower. These are the followers who intuitively understand what the leader needs and get it done, thereby immediately making the leader more effective. These followers are invaluable to the organization and often work hand in hand with the leader. Many future Amplifiers and leaders grew from a behind-the-scenes achiever through a professional development strategy as they learned the ropes of the business. Their desire to remain behind the scenes stems from a combination of their passion to fulfill the mission and their fear of having the responsibility or accountability to make decisions.

Caring/Nurturing

Some followers are motivated by the desire to care for or nurture others. They get a sense of satisfaction out of supporting others and enabling their success. This group of followers is motivated through the accomplishments of others and watching others grow and develop in their careers. Followers of this style can be viewed as parental, because these followers generally take others under their wing. Acting as mentors to many, they seek ways to help others be more effective in their jobs.

Compliant

Compliant followers (subordinates) are those that will get the job done, no more and no less. They do not take initiative beyond the core elements of their defined role or position. These followers are reliable and knowledgeable, and can be counted on to get the job done. Compliant followers do not have career aspirations, or if they do, they are muted. They view their existence as "having a job" and strive to simply show up, get their job done, and head home. Compliant followers play a crucial role when leaders need to get large numbers of employees rowing in the same direction. They are assigned tasks and competently pick them off the list.

Drive and Achievement

Much like many leaders, followers can be motivated by drive and achievement. These are highly competitive followers who have amassed a great deal of skill and accomplishment. They are constantly contributing to the organization in an effort to position themselves for the next promotion or increased sphere of influence. These followers recognize that by enabling the leader's achievements, they will ride that same wave of success.

Higher Purpose

Some followers are motivated by the higher purpose or the mission of the company. They are far less influenced by the leader's style or motives than they are in helping to achieve the mission or purpose of the company. For these followers, it's not what you say but what you stand for, both individually and as an organization. They have little respect for those who aren't on board with passionately driving the mission forward. Because they are passionate about the mission, they can be very helpful in magnifying the organization's culture and conveying the greater message inside and outside of the organization.

Position Player

There are some followers who are passionate about their subject matter expertise and influence but do not want the responsibilities of being a leader. There are a large number of followers who leaders can absolutely rely on but who are not leaders themselves. They do have influence in their particular sphere of influence, but they will take a step back out of the spotlight to let others take the lead.

Servant

Some followers are simply motivated to be the best servant to the organization or their leaders as they can be. They are driven by the purpose or mission of the company and will go to great lengths to accomplish the mission. These followers are motivated beyond the leader and, for as long as there is an ability for them to affect the mission, they will continue to serve.

Work-to-Live

Some followers are outstanding employees who demonstrate many of the traits necessary for them to advance their careers. However, these employees don't actually want a career. They work in order to live. This is their primary motive. When they are engaged, they give 100 percent of their mental capacity and are capable of delivering extraordinary results. These followers are motivated by leaders who respect their boundaries and their work-life balance.

Followership Traits

Followership has a bad rap. Stepping back and scanning the organization, the ratio of people who need to follow are orders of magnitude larger than those who need to lead. It's through followers that companies get the actual work accomplished. When you review this list, you can see why followers are so important to the success of the company. Over the years, we have identified several traits that are prevalent among strong followers and traits that leaders find most valuable among their followers. This is a working list that we keep adjusting as we see greater appreciation of followers and gather feedback from companies as they deploy more effective followership development.

1. **Active/participatory.** Followers take an active role in the evolution and execution of strategies and culture within the company. Good followers do not sit back and wait to be told what to do. They take initiative and play an active role in advancing corporate strategy. These individuals have an insatiable appetite to participate across multiple areas of the organization and advocate for better results. Active followers come up with new ideas, actions, or approaches and bring them forward.

   These followers participate in the core elements and initiatives the company is working on. One of the key traits that followers have is their engagement and active participation in the key elements of the organizations they serve. Followers can't help themselves but to be engaged in the execution or improvement of their companies. Participatory followers are those who contribute their time and effort in strategies, are outspoken during meetings, have suggestions or ask difficult yet constructive questions of management. These followers generally step up in multiple areas of the business to make a difference.

2. **Advisor.** Almost every great leader has at least one trusted advisor. Being an advisor is a special responsibility. To be an effective advisor, one needs to have credibility and knowledge, perspective, insight into the executive's thought process, and the courage to deliver bad news to the leader. The best advisors bring alternative solutions or actions for the leader to consider. Over the years scores of business executives have asked for feedback on one or more of their direct reports in their executive suite. The types and duration of the projects we've performed for them give us a close and upfront view into the leadership, management, and effectiveness of these executives. Clients also value our perspective because we see executives in

similar roles across a number of their peer group companies. Being an advisor to a leader is an extraordinary responsibility. It requires a high-level of discretion and truly objective advice without ulterior motives. The advisor relationship is only possible if it's built on trust. We're grateful when these advisory relationships transcend our projects and exist long after we've completed our work.

3. **Advocate.** In order for companies to make progress and move their organization forward, they need to have a team of supporters advocating for the change or strategy set forth by the leaders. Not all of the strategic choices will be obvious to the broader company. There are the inevitable pitfalls when small teams gather to review the strategy or next steps in the action plan, when the seeds of uncertainty are sown among the group. Advocates step in to keep the positive momentum of the strategy going forward when the leaders are not there to support the effort.

4. **Challenger.** One of the greatest assets good leaders have is a follower who will give honest feedback and is willing to share opinions, especially when they run contrary to the leaders' plan. Leaders need to be challenged in a constructive way, and good followers who serve in the challenger role have the ability to unearth flaws in the leader's thinking, strategy, or approach. Challengers don't take information for granted; they dig deeper to understand the data not being presented as well as the data being presented. They understand differing perspectives and points of view to ensure that they are incorporated into the strategy or approach. Challengers aren't simply being difficult. Rather, they are truly seeking to help build a rock-solid strategy.

5. **Committed.** Good followers are committed to the cause. They may be committed to the organization's vision or purpose, to a particular leader, to their colleagues, to their constituents, or to some combination. But they are committed, nonetheless. Commitment manifests itself in a variety of ways. First and foremost, it can be seen through the dedication to complete the

work at the highest levels of quality. It's visible not just by the quantity of the work being performed but also by the quality of it. Finally, commitment is seen when followers refuse to give up on an assignment until it is completed to the best of their ability. Always resourceful, committed followers solve problems rather than tripping over the inevitable obstacles that arise.

6. **Independent thinker.** The best followers are truly independent thinkers. One of the key areas that gives followership such a bad rap occurs along the dimension of independent thinking. If a leader tries to influence or direct followers to take the wrong action, it's the follower's responsibility to use their independent thinking and judgment to act appropriately. This cannot be confused with consistent disagreement with the leader. Independent thinkers continuously filter all the information presented to them through a critical lens. Further, they are able to bring new and original thoughts and ideas forward to enhance the corporate dialogue on strategy formulation and execution. Independent thinkers do not need to be told what to do at all times. Independent thinkers are more than capable of guiding themselves and their teams consistently with the goals, objectives, and wishes of the leader. Dependent thinkers need constant supervision and direction. They drain managerial resources and do poorly in situations when there is a leadership gap. Therefore, independent thinking among followers serves to advance progress when the risk of stalling exists. Great leaders invite independent thinking to help them make better decisions. Great leaders that are surrounded by "yes" people do not remain great leaders for long.

7. **Learner.** Great followers are lifelong learners. They are constantly absorbing information about their surroundings, their leaders, their colleagues, their companies, and their markets. These learners are studying everything, with special emphasis on what to do and what *not* to do. The follower learners have an insatiable appetite to learn new job skills, management techniques, leadership capabilities, human behavior,

and how markets work. They have a clear recognition that their success rests in part on their job competency and in part on how they lead and how they carry out the work of the leaders they follow.

8. **Motivational.** Followers often play the role of the surrogate motivator. Frequently the leaders who set the direction or embark on transformation efforts are not close to the day-to-day operations of the company. It is therefore up to their key followers, and their followers' followers, to amplify the leader's message and motivate the broader organization to carry out and execute the stated strategy. There are times that organizations have a particular leadership gap at the top. When this occurs, followers have a special opportunity to motivate the company and fill the leadership void.

9. **Principled.** Great followers have a set of unwavering principles that guide their behavior and the behavior they expect of their leaders and others. In companies with strong cultures, they embrace a set of core values based on principles. Unfortunately, we saw in the Volkswagen emissions scandal that employees without principles placed their job security or personal gain ahead of the simple evaluation of right and wrong. When a principled follower is confronted with unethical behavior, they confront the offender. Principled followers in groups have the power to create a culture that will not permit unethical leadership practices to exist. Principled followers have a tremendous sense of right and wrong and apply moral compass as the guiding force in their decision-making. This in turn refines the leaders' perspectives and sharpens their leadership skills.

10. **Reliable.** Reliability is a core character strength for followers. Leaders can count on followers to carry out the assignments they need completed in a timely and effective manner. Good followers reliably deliver. Furthermore, they create a culture of delivery excellence where their teams join together to increase the predictability that the tasks and outcomes will be delivered in an effective and timely way.

11. **Responsible/Accountable.** Good followers take their responsibility to another level. They feel committed and responsible to deliver on the stated mission and purpose of the company, while doing so in a way that creates an environment that is rewarding and engaging for their colleagues. When tasked with assignments, followers take on the responsibility and shoulder the burden to get the job done. These followers generate a sense of accomplishment as they complete the work under their charge.

    Responsible followers also take accountability for issues or mistakes they make along the way or for less than par performance among their teams. They proactively step forward in a responsible manner to correct the situation and team members involved. They do not shirk responsibility and are accountable to their leaders and other followers alike.

12. **Servant.** Being a good follower requires all the elements of being a good servant. There have been a number of books written about servant leadership that are worth reading. Good followers not only serve their leaders but also they serve their followers. It is a selfless endeavor and one in which they are constantly seeking to better understand the needs of those they serve. When they anticipate the needs before they are even known and offer answers to those questions or ideas to solve a problem, the servant follower is an invaluable asset.

13. **Teacher.** One of the personality traits common for good followers is their passion to share their knowledge to help others grow and learn. Good followers are lifelong learners themselves, and they have a particular soft spot for teaching others what they know. Over the years, one of the common threads contained in the conversations I've had with leaders is how proud they are when people they've mentored have gone on to do great things. Rarely do I hear the long list of accomplishments that they themselves have had. What they share with me instead are the numerous people they've mentored and how far those individuals have progressed in their own careers.

14. **Visionary.** In order to be an effective follower and be an advisor to leaders, it's necessary to have certain anticipatory or visionary skills. These are essential in the strategic game theory and what-if choices necessary to create effective strategies. Anticipating the next several steps necessary to forecast the quarters or years ahead is essential in helping the leader frame the road map required for an organization to achieve sustainable success.

8 Amplifier Styles, Motives, and Traits

Amplifiers exist at the intersection of highly capable leaders and exemplary followers. These highly capable and valuable employees exist throughout the organization. The best-run companies know how to spot these star professionals. But it is amazing how some organizations lack the fundamental insights into their employee base to even know where to find these amazing contributors. This intersection presents a unique breed of contributor, and companies that identify, nurture, and advance these Amplifiers will outperform their competitors.

Amplifier Styles

Because Amplifiers combine the best of leadership and followership into one person, they are typically at the top of leadership development succession pipelines. Sometimes this is masked through their leadership capabilities, but it is the unique blend that really sets them apart as their own breed. Amplifiers are great followers who have high career aspirations and the leadership capability to ascend in the organization to take on ever-increasing levels of responsibility. Our experience working with the highest-performing global companies highlights the following Amplifier styles of their leaders, listed in Table 8.1.

Table 8.1   Amplifier Styles

---

1. Activator
2. Anticipator
3. Handler
4. Magnifier
5. Radiant
6. Trusted advisor/skeptic

Activator

Activators are Amplifiers who have the ability to energize colleagues to take action and start a journey or task. The activator is an amazing contributor to the organization. They activate the masses to lead change and deliver on major transformation efforts. Activators know where in the organization the "real" work gets done and the leaders they can rely on to get others to follow the stated strategy. Organizational transformation efforts need to employ these activators. More than just change agents, these activators can lead the masses to accomplish the goals.

Anticipator

The anticipator brings the unique combination of clairvoyance and practical execution of the present tasks. Amplifiers who can anticipate future strategic moves and incorporate them into the current workload are able to best position the firm for future success. This style needs to incorporate elements of strategic and visionary thinking while integrating it into the flow of current activities.

Handler

The handler is an Amplifier who handles a function, project, task, or activity for a leader. The handler may be the leader assigned to transform an underperforming business unit, lead an acquisition integration, and so on. The most effective senior leaders always have their set of handlers for various initiatives. These types of Amplifiers often proactively identify a need and volunteer to take care of it, long before it is identified as needing an assigned owner by the leader. Handlers simply take the ball and run with it, announcing they will handle it and competently deliver the results back to the group without much fanfare.

Magnifier

Some Amplifiers have the ability to magnify the results of any particular goal, objective, or initiative. Once they are responsible for leading a portion of the effort, they find ways to improve it and make it even more effective and impactful for the organization and its constituents. These Amplifiers are creative, resourceful, and innovative. Magnifiers seem to amplify the strengths or positive natures of the firm or its people while shoring up the weaknesses.

Radiant

True Amplifiers have a dynamic and radiant presence. They have a unique magnetism that draws others in to work with them and want to be part of the initiatives they are part of. Like charismatic leaders, this style displays a level of optimism and can-do attitude that is infectious; yet radiant Amplifiers emanate substance and depth of expertise. Radiant Amplifiers never seem to get shaken during times of stress. They possess a presence and demeanor that exudes confidence and creates a safe space for the team to overcome any obstacle in their path.

Trusted Advisor/Skeptic

Many of the CEOs we have interacted with have been a trusted advisor or trusted skeptic for a former CEO. They will share in small or personal settings what the leader really needs to know to make better decisions. They reveal blind spots to these leaders, with a constructive eye toward shedding light on their weaknesses and changing behavior. Because they are able to provide insight into the leader's thinking, oftentimes other leaders will engage these trusted advisors to vet ideas prior to presenting to the leader. Many leaders will skip a level (or in some cases go to a lower level in the company) to gather the feedback they need. These individuals are the go-to people when issues confront the organization. They are the people in the room with little power, but many times, the most information.

Amplifier Motives

Amplifiers are driven by personal and professional motives. Generally speaking, Amplifiers are inspired by similar motives as leaders and followers. Amplifiers are career-oriented and not only want to serve their constituents in order to achieve the company's mission but also grow their careers. It is this unique blend that enables them to magnify outcomes. They have high standards and low levels of acceptance for people who don't carry their weight.

Unlike titled executives or passive subordinates, Amplifiers are driven by altruistic motives. They are passionate about and motivated to achieve excellence with an ever-increasing standard of service and level of performance. Amplifiers prefer to associate with other Amplifiers, regardless of title or level. They draw energy from and exude energy to other Amplifiers. In this way, they magnify the power of teams in order to unleash even greater levels of performance.

Achievement

Most Amplifiers are aware of their ability and influence as they progress their careers. As they gain success in role after role, they start to feed off of the recognition and results they are delivering for the company and their colleagues. They are motivated to achieve higher levels of performance and obtain greater responsibility. For the most part, Amplifiers seek rewards and recognition commensurate with the results they produce and the achievements they deliver.

Apprentice/Successor

There is an interesting relationship among Amplifiers, the leaders they learn from, and the followers they teach. This link creates a master-apprentice relationship in which knowledge and methods are demonstrated from the leader to the follower and again to more followers in turn. As leaders are promoted in their careers, they turn to the people who help them achieve their success whether directly or indirectly and promote them as well. These Amplifiers are motivated to follow in the footsteps of their successful leaders, and they seek out new leaders to follow if they are reporting to a titled executive.

Over a long professional career, many leaders evolve from being takers in the early days to being givers later in their careers. If nurtured throughout an organization, this dynamic can create a healthy culture. In this regenerative leadership and followership dynamic, organizations can pass on healthy habits and behaviors to the next generation of leaders. True Amplifiers are willing to challenge or question if they are unsure of the leader's guidance. This can work only if they have the trust and respect of the leader and their colleagues. Furthermore, their motives need to be in the right place. But under this backdrop, the role of the trusted skeptic is an essential role for any leader. Ironically, it is these Amplifiers who are also studied by others in the organization. Oftentimes, Amplifiers are actively seeking their own professional growth subconsciously while developing others. In doing so, they may lose sight of the fact that others are following in their wake with the same fervor that the Amplifier is following in the leader's wake.

Excellence

All Amplifiers are motivated to achieve even greater levels of excellence. They need to constantly improve and not rest on their laurels; this motivation is what drives these professionals to perpetually improve their surroundings and how the company operates. The need for excellence is demonstrated in their action and becomes contagious. Amplifiers have a low tolerance for subpar or lazy performance by their followers. They want to work on teams and select colleagues to work with them that are similarly motivated to achieve excellence in everything they do. They have a high bar for themselves in the organization so if they themselves are not rising up the ranks they will view themselves as a failure.

Navigator

Navigators are motivated to climb the corporate ladder through their own results and the results they can achieve through others. They are politically savvy and understand how to lead and manage up as well as down and throughout the organization. Amplifiers who are motivated to navigate thorny situations do so in order to advance the common good of the organization as well as their own career success.

Purpose

Many Amplifiers are simply driven by the company's mission or higher purpose. They have little regard for internal politics, perception, or other factors that may slow them down from delivering on the purpose. They possess independent and critical thinking skills, deep subject matter expertise, and competence, and they have the influence necessary to lead up, down, and across the organization. As a result, they accomplish extraordinary results without any expectation for recognition. Their heads are in the sand so to speak while they pursue the ultimate purpose. For as long as the company supports them in their mission, they will remain engaged and deliver superior results individually and through the teams they oversee.

Recognition

Some Amplifiers are motivated by the internal and external recognition they achieve from the results of their actions or the actions of the teams they lead. They are energized by seeing their name in lights and all the related appreciation that they receive. These professionals have a high need for achievement, coupled with a high need of positive affirmation.

Amplifier Traits

True Amplifiers possess special character traits that enable them to magnify the power of teams and increase the impact of the company. They are a special blend of strong leadership and followership traits. Every strong leader develops their career experiences through a combination of being a leader and a follower. Over time, they exemplify leadership, followership, or both traits simultaneously. Amplifier traits can be developed through training and learning teams. It takes a conscious effort to identify the trait and develop the corresponding skills associated with it. The following traits are borne from our experience working with top leaders of companies and learning from their experience as they ascended their careers.

1. **Anticipation.** One of the most important character traits of an Amplifier is what we call *strategic anticipation,* which occurs when the Amplifier helps to envision forces that will affect the performance of the organization in the future. These can be internal forces, competitive forces, or even existential threats. What's tricky about these challenges is that they need to be understood well enough to build the case for change. One challenge people have when they present a case for change is that it needs to have substance. Amplifiers have a keen sense of the critical issues confronting an organization and possess the essential trait of strategic anticipation. Corporate performance hinges on its collective ability to anticipate critical decisions that may stand in the way of an organization reaching its full potential. Amplifiers frame the conversation so clearly that these decisions can be made in a timely fashion.

2. **Authentic.** Authenticity is a hallmark for Amplifiers. They are true to their beliefs and are willing to speak truth to power. They bring their authentic selves to work and bring out the best of each and everyone's unique talents. There is a motto that guides authentic Amplifier behavior and that is, to thine own self be true. When their heads hit their pillows at night, they know that they have left it all on the field. There are no regrets, no stones unturned, no loose ends to be tied up. Individuals who possess this character trait have a reputation that their word can be trusted, their motives are pure, and their actions are genuinely in the best interest of the stakeholders.

3. **Brave/Courageous.** Having the courage to step out and speak truth to power, present a differing point of view or unpopular perspective, or represent an underappreciated group of colleagues is not always embraced by leadership. Necessarily, this requires bravery. But to Amplifiers steadfast in their authentic purpose, it is the only right thing to do. Effective leaders who have risen in their careers and have developed this skill make it safe for brave Amplifiers to speak their minds and share their alternative strategies. When confronted with titled executives, brave Amplifiers are in a lonely spot; but instead of fleeing or quitting, they embrace the challenge and confront leadership.

4. **Contribution seekers.** One of the most interesting character traits of Amplifiers is their constant search for new ways they can add value and contribute to the organization's success. Many times, they have a full workload and are actively engaged in many aspects of the business and strategic initiatives. Yet somehow, they seem to find new ways that they can help. Contribution seekers don't complain about lack of time. They have learned how to channel time to their advantage and leverage others to get work done. Over the years, throughout our engagements with clients, we have seen several effective processes or strategies that they have put into place. We are always curious where these innovative process improvements originate. Oftentimes we learn that someone in the field created

a better and more effective way to get something done. Alternatively, we hear stories about these Amplifiers who were observing colleagues struggling to perform activities related to but not directly in their group. They stepped in to help those colleagues despite the extra workload, even though many times there wasn't a reward for going above and beyond. They were motivated instead by knowing it was for the common good and that the entire organization would benefit.

5. **Creativity.** True Amplifiers get creative when confronted with unique challenges. They don't stop and wait for direction; they poke and prod and explore alternative means to solve the problem. These Amplifiers become quite resourceful and deploy an entrepreneurial and enterprising mindset to think through the challenges at hand. They take initiative and don't let the roadblocks they encounter stop progress. They take it further by removing barriers and solving problems in a creative way. Finding creative solutions and incorporating them into daily operations is a valuable skill that Amplifiers possess.

6. **Discretion.** One of the most valuable character traits possessed by Amplifiers is discretion. Leaders need Amplifiers whom they can absolutely trust, and discretion is at the heart of that trust. There are many critical issues that confront a business leader, and they need to bounce around ideas that are not yet formed with key Amplifiers prior to those ideas getting incorporated into a major decision. Before a cake is baked, it is half-baked; so it is with strategies and major decisions. Many good strategies get derailed because their half-baked elements get out prematurely. This is also true as it relates to succession planning, M&A, restructurings, and other critical and highly sensitive decisions.

7. **Grace.** During our research on Amplifiers, one of the interesting character traits that emerged was grace. Grace is not a typical business-oriented character trait. The best leaders, followers, and Amplifiers display grace in all aspects of what they do. All good leaders get passed up for a promotion, make mistakes,

or fail. Leaders also experience and own the mistakes and failures of their followers. Grace is acknowledging these setbacks or failures in a calm and reassuring manner. Acting with grace also makes it safe for followers to acknowledge their mistakes, which in turn creates a safe environment for all to develop and improve.

Another demonstration of grace is displayed in the guilelessness leaders show in the ordinary course of business. The famous author Henry Drummond in *The Greatest Thing in the World* defines guilelessness as "the grace for suspicious people. The possession of it is the great secret of personal influence." He goes on, "You will find the people who most influence you are those who believe in you. In an atmosphere of suspicion, people shrivel up; but in an atmosphere of grace they expand, and find encouragement, and educative fellowship."[1] It is in this environment that true Amplifiers excel and create the comradery necessary for extraordinary performance.

8. **Healthy skepticism.** Many organizations are filled with Monday morning quarterbacks. What makes Amplifiers special is that they present their challenges to their leader from a healthy place. They are a trusted skeptic. The trusted skeptic has been granted the authority by their leaders to attempt to pierce their strategies or plans, shoot holes in them, and help ensure they are better in the end.

Amplifiers have a knack for relying on the concept of "trust but verify." It's one thing to be skeptical about information presented or a particular approach being pushed from the top. But healthy skepticism is a far more productive attitude and is rooted in what is best for the organization. If something doesn't seem right or doesn't smell right, it's worth digging into. Amplifiers will dig into certain aspects of corporate strategy or policies that don't seem right.

9. **Humility.** True Amplifiers learn not to think less of themselves but to think of themselves less. This definition of humility subrogates the will of the Amplifier for those whom they are

serving. Amplifiers recognize that they are only as strong as the people around them and that they are far better served by supporting them. Paradoxically, the more support Amplifiers provide for others, the more support they in turn receive. Great leaders who possess humility, especially Level 5 leaders, demonstrate to and nurture humility in their followers.

Amplifiers have an honest and true understanding of their talents and weaknesses. Because their egos do not get in the way, they are able to use this honest assessment to add value where they can and tap other resources when they need to. They don't try to pretend to possess skills they don't have. They rely on leverage in relationships to find it in other parts of the company. Usually this is readily given as Amplifiers themselves are frequently tapped by others for their expertise.

Humility surfaces as one of the most important character traits that Amplifiers place on the leaders they follow and it's one of the most important traits for them to be known for among their own followers. One of the best ways to be a humble leader is to remember the age-old adage that you were given two eyes, two ears, and one mouth for a reason: to observe and listen twice as much as you talk. It's hard to be extremely self-centered and humble at the same time. This is why the charisma trap is so important for leaders to continually monitor. Given that self-interest erodes trust, as demonstrated in Charlie Green's trust equation, we created the humility equation.

10. **Inclusivity.** Amplifiers are very inclusive in their approach to diversity of thought and participation, equity, and inclusion. They recognize that mobilizing a broader group of individuals will produce superior results and have a deeper impact on the organization. They also have a learning mindset when it comes to bias that exists individually or at a corporate level. In my interview with him, Hassinger shared how he's developed over the years to better appreciate gender and racial bias in the workplace. When he started working forty years ago, the professional environment had a widely different view than it has

today. There's been significant progress in this regard, yet we have only begun to scratch the surface. Part of what shaped his perspective has been his global experience. Being responsible for leading employees in different parts of the world necessitates an awareness of cultural and societal norms. He also acknowledged that this experience has helped shape his perspective and shined a light on his views.

11. **Intuition.** Amplifiers develop a sharply honed sixth sense, a level of intuition that sets them apart from their peers. They have the ability to intuitively know the needs of their followers, leaders, and the broader organization. Furthermore, they take these intuitive thoughts and incorporate them into the active strategies being carried out by the company. Intuition leads to the proper formulation of a vision. It also comes into play when people say they have a good "gut feel" about a situation. A strong intuition leads to further probing, exploration, fact-finding, and decision framing necessary for the company to deliver its best work. Sometimes that requires patience to continue to seek answers until that clarity is revealed.

12. **Judgment.** The ability to objectively reach a conclusion using good judgment, especially when all facts are not known, is one of the key characteristics of Amplifiers. Amplifiers set the decision-making tone by displaying good judgment over time. By doing this, they influence their colleagues and create a supporting environment to amplify good judgment across teams in the organization.

13. **Learner.** Amplifiers are lifelong learners. One particular aspect of Amplifiers is that they are students of others, learning from some what to do and from others what not to do. There is a particular magnetism they have with the leaders who will invest time in their knowledge to show them the ropes, expose them to different aspects of the business, and share how they arrive at their decisions. The energy Amplifiers provide for their leaders and the leaders' energy for the Amplifiers become a virtuous cycle in which both parties draw strength and derive

substantial benefits. They are constantly seeking to develop and grow professionally and personally. This is not to be confused with the individual seeking out certifications or degrees simply to pad their résumé. The knowledge sought by Amplifiers oftentimes is on their own time or is part of apprentice-style learning from an expert at a firm where there is no certificate. This true pursuit of development is based on their passion to exceed and produce to serve the organization or the company's mission to their best ability and is not based on selfish motives. Amplifiers also have a keen sense for what they don't know and are adept at finding people who have that knowledge or particular talent.

One of the common characteristics of Amplifiers is their learning style. Whereas they all have had numerous internal and external training or professional development courses, they seem to recall only a few that made a genuine impact. However, these Amplifiers have found that what they believe to be most impactful is the informal peer-to-peer groups getting together to go over particular topics and learn from each other. In this small-group setting, among three or four peers with a common goal, one idea triggers another and the healthy banter creates a learning pod that leads to more effective absorption of the content. The other way Amplifiers learn is by working with their leaders. They are apprentices in their lifelong quest to grow professionally in all aspects of their career development.

14. **Leverage.** One of the interesting character traits that emerged from our research for leaders and exemplary followers is their ability to leverage other people or resources to accomplish the objectives of the organization. These Amplifiers have a special way of getting more done than ordinary employees. Many times, they do so without the direct authority over the staff members who perform the job. Instead, they are able to accomplish this through influence. There always seems to be more work or ideas than there are people to carry them out. Amplifiers understand leverage.

They also understand reverse leverage, which is the art of getting work done by your leader/boss or other executives at the company. Great leaders understand and grant the authority to Amplifiers to accomplish aspects of the strategy or execute the strategic plan. Over the years, when interacting with executives who are great leaders themselves, it's no surprise to hear the stories about an Amplifier who delivers a prepackaged decision for the leader. The tight bond that the Amplifier and leader develop together enables the Amplifier to fully understand the information necessary for the leader to make the decision. They deliver the decision package to the leader's desk and without much fanfare the call is made. The efficiency of this interchange is extraordinary for the leader and the Amplifier. On the other side of the spectrum, Amplifiers recognize the power of what they can accomplish by motivating and encouraging others to get the work done. This can be done within their teams, but oftentimes it's done in a broader cross-functional or cross-regional way.

15. **Listener.** Listening is a key trait essential for organizational success. One of the mistakes leaders make when communicating their decisions is that at times, they can be tone deaf. The art of listening is broken into three areas. First, leaders and Amplifiers are passionate about listening to the voices of the customer, their employees, regulators, the supply chain, shareholders, and so on. Frequently, leaders focus on what is actually said. It is essential to get direct feedback from these constituents, good or bad. Companies invest a lot of time and resources to capture this information and synthesize it into actionable initiatives to magnify strengths and shore up weaknesses. It's important that they ask the right questions, or they will only receive a partial view of the information necessary. The second element that is essential to listening is the art of hearing what is not said. We've learned over the years to spot certain catchphrases that people say to masquerade true intent. Their words are less debatable and for a novice listener, they are taken at face value and they

move on. Or in other cases, they are a softer way to let the person down. The Amplifier has the ability to read between the lines and understand the speaker's true intent in the context of the literal remarks. Finally, Amplifiers have a keen sense of when a decision or action to be communicated will be met with a wide range of mixed support. In this case, the Amplifier is able to effectively "listen ahead" to anticipate the reaction, acknowledging the reluctance and rationale upfront. This ability to listen ahead dramatically reduces the chance that an unpopular decision will be communicated in a tone-deaf manner.

16. **Magnetism.** True Amplifiers are magnetic. They themselves create a following. But interestingly, these Amplifiers attract leaders to invest time in them. Leaders are reluctant to invest time in people whom they don't see participate in the process. When they find true followers, who are passionate to learn and grow, leaders will take the extra time and energy necessary to develop them professionally. Leaders gravitate to people who want to get better. The longer that leaders have been at the job, the more they are able to intuitively know how to peg a return on their time invested in the follower. Therefore, if they don't see that a follower will coinvest with them in the follower's development, the leader will move on to those who will. One of the scarcest resources leaders have is their time. However, the magnetism of a true Amplifier and their willingness to engage in the development process will have the ability to pull in multiple leaders to help propel these Amplifiers' careers.

17. **Mindfulness.** One of the interesting character traits that came forward in our research is mindfulness. Historically, mindfulness has not been one of the common leadership traits that has been assigned to great leaders. Leaders need to understand that they are constantly under the microscope. Followers watch what leaders are doing and how they're acting even when the leader does not recognize they are being watched. Amplifiers magnify this trait as they lead by example and bridge the gap among other followers. Amplifiers are aware at all times

of how their actions and behaviors affect others. Mindfulness is the leader's ability to intuitively take actions while mentally sifting through dozens of strategic initiatives and thousands of considerations for each. Despite how cluttered their minds are with all these thoughts, Amplifiers continue to take the time to listen and observe their surroundings so that they can lead by example. Generally, leaders are in a rush if their hands are full, but when they stop and hold the door for someone, people take note.

Mindfulness is the conscious state of being aware of the current surroundings and the present moment while acknowledging the prevailing circumstances as they are. There are too many examples when companies turn a blind eye on a particular situation. It is, in essence, corporate denial of a strategic or cultural character defect. Amplifiers who are mindful of the corporate culture and current state of affairs are better able to incorporate these realities into corporate strategy or transformation efforts. Transformation efforts fail in part because leaders are not mindful of the actual starting point of the organization. In some cases, they will try to survey the company, but if they are not mindful, they cannot be good listeners, and thus they will likely start off in the wrong direction of the journey.

Over the years, we have worked with companies large and small. Unfortunately, too frequently we will leave one of our long roll-up-your-sleeve workshop visioning sessions, and one of our client counterparts will say something to the effect of, "There is no way that team is capable of executing on that, but sadly the manager really believes they can." There is a lot to unpack in this quote but at its core is the absence of mindfulness and the potential consequences of taking action based on a false premise.

Simply because an organization is mindful of its current circumstances does not mean it needs to accept them as tomorrow's foregone conclusion. Quite the opposite is true. Being mindful of the current state of affairs and with institutional humility, the organization can set out to create the change necessary to arrive at the next stop along the enterprise's destination journey.

18. **Optimistic.** The best Amplifiers are optimistic. Because there are always setbacks, Amplifiers recognize that optimism is the fuel for resilience. Amplifiers are constantly dealing with direct or indirect challenges, which can create fear, uncertainty, and doubt. But the Amplifiers' optimism enables their followers to continue marching down the path. That said, Amplifiers must achieve the right balance of optimism and reality. Too much optimism can lead to exaggeration, and exaggeration is an eroding force of credibility for effective leadership.

19. **Resourcefulness.** The best Amplifiers are able find ways to add value across a broad spectrum of activities whether or not they have direct control of the financial or human resources. Amplifiers have the influence and wherewithal to assemble the resources necessary to accomplish the goal. This requires creativity, influence, and competence in order to assemble the right components of a winning strategy.

20. **Standard setters.** Amplifiers have a high bar for personal and organizational excellence and are standard setters for others. True Amplifiers constantly raise the bar and set new and higher standards for the organization to follow. They seem to find new ways to add value, root out waste, reinvent poor processes, optimize talent, and generally optimize the parts of the organization that they oversee. For many long-established companies, it's amazing to see how a business function or department that has been operating in a particular way for years changes and reinvents itself when an Amplifier is assigned to oversee the group. They have a way of making the impossible possible. The injection of fresh talent at the top has a way of reinvigorating the entire team. When they progress to their next roles, their successors are left with a far better starting place in a stronger team to make continuous improvements.

    As beacons of standards for excellence, Amplifiers struggle with others' lazy and sloppy work. There are a few aspects of the Amplifier personality that generate a visceral negative response: one is cutting corners and producing less than full-potential work. These are pet peeves of most standard setters. When subordinates genuinely need the help, this help is gladly given. Standard setters are demanding, yet fair. But sustained laziness and marginal performance is unacceptable to Amplifiers. This applies to their team members, as well as others within the organization, which can include leaders. Their expectations hold beyond their core team or sphere of influence and they feel that a bad example in a different group is a poor reflection on the company as a whole.

21. **Synthesizer.** The synthesizer trait is one of the most valuable Amplifier traits that yields substantial returns for the company. Synthesizers bring together all of the elements necessary to breathe life into a strategy. Virtually all strategic initiatives or transformation efforts require the careful orchestration of activities and resources that exist internally and externally throughout the organization. Coordinating all these activities to ensure that the effort is successful requires the artful execution of the synthesizer trait. This is true not just for the leader in the top spot; synthesizers are needed throughout the entire team to carry out the strategic project. Many times, these key team members need to pull resources or get work done outside of their direct control. That work hits the critical path and needs to be woven into the overall project or transformation effort.

22. **Teacher.** Just as Amplifiers are exceptional students and learners, they are equally passionate about teaching and developing others. Amplifiers place a high value on knowledge and outcomes that are aligned with the organization's purpose and mission. As a result, they have a vested stake in imparting knowledge to their followers in order for the whole organization to be more effective at what they do. Great leaders also tap into Amplifiers to help them shore up their knowledge gaps. They invite the follower to teach them aspects of the business

where they have not been as deeply exposed as they ascended in their career.

23. **Visionary.** Amplifiers have the vision necessary to see a future that their teams, and the company as a whole, can aspire to achieve, and they have a sense of how to get there. Followers want to know where their leaders are taking the organization. They want to know not only the destination but also their purpose. Therefore, it is critical that Amplifiers articulate their vision in such a way that inspires followers to take action. It is also important that this vision is aligned toward some higher purpose. One of the things that erodes the momentum of change is when an organization has a shallowness of purpose. Employees in these types of organizations feel they have "just a job" and that they are not on a mission to achieve something of greater good. The other element we found is the concept of bravery or courageousness. Not all strategic choices along the way are easy choices to make. They require calculated risks, which in turn requires the bravery to know when to take them. Most employees in an organization are pragmatic followers and by definition do not want to take risks. This is where Amplifiers play a critical role in executing a leader's vision.

24. **Vulnerability.** Being vulnerable is not a sign of weakness but paradoxically a demonstration of strength. Amplifiers understand that being honest with and critical of themselves regarding their strengths and weaknesses actually inspires followers to do the same. This leads to more productive outcomes than trying to hide or cover up their weaknesses. We see that when fear grips leaders. They are afraid that by admitting to a mistake they will lose followers, or their ego will not look good, or they will not achieve a particular reward or recognition. Rather, when leaders admit to a mistake or that they don't know something, they create more followers. This is especially true when the followers understand that the leaders have learned from the mistake or, in the case of a capability gap, they've assigned the right person with the requisite

skills necessary to solve the problem. When leaders own their mistakes publicly, the organization sees that it is safe to make a mistake so that the team can focus on fixing the mistake instead of the fallout of a cover-up.

Example of Mindfulness

Early in my career as an entry-level consultant assigned to work on an engagement for Marriott at their corporate headquarters, I was a junior staffer thirsty to learn and study not only the business but also the people behind the businesses. At the time, Marriott was in the business of providing the service and hospitality for hotels. One of their most significant lines of business was providing cafeteria services for corporate customers. They used their own cafeteria as an example and when potential customers came for sales calls, instead of going out for a fancy lunch, which was common at the time, the sales team would host their prospects at the corporate cafeteria. One day as I was working my way through the cafeteria, a large entourage of executive management of the prospective customer as well as senior executives at Marriott came through. I paused and watched the scene play out. Among the hustle and bustle of the busy cafeteria someone must've dropped their tray or something as there was a decent sized mess on the floor by one of the stations. People walked around it as they were filling their trays. It was then that I noticed Bill Marriott himself quietly and without uttering a word put his tray down at one of the stations, grabbed a rag and got on his hands and knees in his suit to clean up the mess. Again, without saying a word, he picked up his tray and continued along getting his lunch, rejoining the executives. It seems the cafeteria manager also saw what had just happened and I watched as he proceeded to scold his subordinates. Bill Marriott did not need to say one word. He knew his actions were far more powerful. He grew up in the business and knew that service was the key to success. No tasks were too small for him to perform himself as he did when he was growing up in the business. It was a teaching opportunity not just for the cafeteria crew but also for his direct reports who also ignored the mess. It clearly had a big impact on me, as I'm recounting the story more than thirty years later.

We have seen others call mindfulness "situational awareness." When Steve Jobs told Indra Nooyi to throw a temper tantrum, she knew not to do it all the time.[2] But being mindful of the situation, she knew when doing so would create the best results. Alternatively, letting your temper flash and inappropriately lashing out has equally lasting negative effects.

Amplifiers
in Action

9

Amplifying Corporate Strategy

True Amplifiers increase the impact of organizations. Organizational impact is measured through the lens of value created for its stakeholders. Not all stakeholder value is created equally. One of the most important factors in creating corporate strategy is to fully understand the stakeholder value and time horizon of the strategy. Stakeholders include shareholders, employees, customers, and the societies in which they operate. Companies play a vital role in the economic engine that drive worldwide economies and raise the standard of living for all. The Business Roundtable recently adjusted its statement of purpose of a corporation to be more in line with the values of all stakeholders, not just shareholders.[1] We believe effective corporate strategy takes a long-term view of the benefits for the stakeholders, and doing so creates an environment for companies to thrive well into the future.

The rate of change in the global economic environment continues to accelerate at breakneck speed. In this rapidly changing business climate, Amplifiers are playing an increasingly important role by constantly feeding data, insights, and other information into strategy formulation within their companies. It's impossible for leaders of large organizations to have a firm grasp on all of the market forces and details that affect strategy. Leaders cannot be successful without appropriately leveraging all the human resources at their disposal.

Some leaders call this "returning authority," when certain decisions are expected to be made closer to the front lines by followers who are closest to the fact pattern.

It's always been amazing to me to see how many different strategic frameworks have been published over the years. There are hundreds of books on strategy, most of which are pitching a particular strategic framework, method, or process for the company to follow. In our consulting business, we also have particular models that we deploy on a situational basis for different strategy engagements for our industry clients. Over the years, we found that what works best is to layer in different concepts from different models depending on the emphasis of the strategy. But regardless of the model used, the single common element of all good strategy projects is the human element and rigorous thought.

One of the fascinating elements of watching corporate strategy development unfold is how the organization experiences the "journey of the strategy." For most people in the organization, when a leader articulates future strategy, it is as if they're standing on the South rim of the Grand Canyon unsure how to get to the North rim. The journey of the strategy is how the organization adjusts, adapts, learns, grows, and repositions the product or geographic portfolio, teams, and resources to get there. Frequently, these multiyear strategy efforts are launched with much fanfare. As the strategy unfolds over the ensuing time periods, fatigue starts to set in across the organization. Successful leaders need to understand this natural occurrence and nurture the organization along so that the proper pace can be maintained, enriched by leadership along the journey.

There are four key elements to effective corporate strategy. At every level, it is the human element that shapes the effectiveness of that strategy.

1. **The quality of the strategy itself.** The creation and the quality of the strategy is an output of human analysis, research, scenario planning, visioning, and other activities to create the strategy.

Amplifiers have a keen sense for the needs of all stakeholders and how to incorporate these needs into the strategic plan.

2. **The execution of the strategy.** It doesn't matter how good the strategy is if the company cannot execute. A good strategy and a good execution of that strategy need to come together for an organization to be successful. At the heart of strategic execution are the people in the organization, not the strategy itself. An organization that develops a brilliant strategy that it can't execute will suboptimize stakeholder value.

3. **The sustainability of the strategy over time.** Understanding the sustainability of a particular strategy is also critical. Some companies believe they are innovative, yet they pursue an acquisition strategy instead of creating an innovative culture. This works until the company is faced with massive goodwill and debt on the balance sheet.

4. **The agility of the strategy to accommodate strategic shifts.** Great companies are able to pivot quickly and adjust to key market forces. They have built agility into their strategic processes. This is obviously far more difficult in heavily capital–intensive businesses with long product development cycles, but, nonetheless, strategic agility to capitalize on an emerging trend, or disengage a particular line of business, is a key element that separates great companies from good companies.

According to McKinsey & Company, 70 percent of transformation efforts fail.[2] This is a striking statistic and leads us to ask several questions. How is success measured? Why do these transformation efforts fail? If so many transformation efforts fail, why do executives pursue them with the fervor that they do? Reviewing data from earnings calls and investor presentations reveals that almost all companies are pursuing a stated strategy. Does this mean that 70 percent of the Fortune 500 are pursuing a strategy destined for failure? Why do the 30 percent succeed? What do these 30 percent have in common? We believe the answer to this last question rests in how they activate Amplifiers to influence strategy formulation and execution.

Organizations measure success in a variety of ways. For many companies, they measure success by financial metrics such as market share, growth rates, or stock price performance. Other purpose-driven organizations measure patients served, life-saving therapeutics brought to market, or other societal benefits delivered to their constituents.

There is a vast array of strategic frameworks that exist. Some have been popularized over the years by major brand-name consulting firms. One example is the strategy of being number one, two, or three in an industry. This strategy was pursued by a number of *former* great companies. American Airlines flew itself into bankruptcy and was acquired by US Airways. Chrysler drove itself into the ground and was acquired. IBM rested on its laurels and failed to innovate. The transformation challenge at such a large conglomerate is significant. Nokia transformed itself over the course of a century, but after they ascended to the top of the smartphone market, seemingly achieving the stated strategy of being the top player in the market, they fell precipitously. Some of the biggest and well-funded number one, two, and three brewers of beer missed the craft brewing craze entirely. They were swept up in their own strategic echo chamber only to miss the trend. To be sure, these organizations had some great leaders at the helm, but despite spending tens of millions of dollars on strategy, they failed to recognize what was eroding their success. In some cases, they were able to recover and thrive, but in other cases they have fallen into obscurity.

Why does this highly touted business school strategic philosophy fail so frequently? And why do so many companies still pursue it? No doubt, scale is helpful, but it is not essential for long-term success. In fact, evidence shows that being number one, two, or three in a market is far from guaranteeing long-term success. What then separates those who maintain the top spots and continue to execute well over time? There is some evidence that hubris can exist at the corporate level as well as the individual level. When this mindset is fixed in the employees of the firm, it hampers the ability for true Amplifiers to emerge.

Another common strategy is an untethered pursuit of growth for growth's sake. These acquisitive companies bought other companies, leveraging their balance sheets along the way. The amassing of goodwill to fund growth can work only in environments of low interest rates and rising stock prices. This strategy does produce growth, and when executive compensation rewards growth, this strategy is expensive for long-term stockholders. There are endless examples of companies that grew through acquisition but could not produce organic growth. When an existential shock hits the market, these companies fall from grace quickly.

We saw this strategy unravel recently during the global COVID-19 pandemic. Many companies, especially those in retail, who borrowed significantly to acquire companies for growth, were unable to survive the revenue shock caused by store closures. Companies with a strong balance sheet were able to withstand the disruption brought about by widespread shutdowns. There were surprising stumbles by companies not immediately thought of as at-risk because of the shutdown.

If 70 percent of transformation efforts fail, why do leaders embark on them? There are several reasons why business leaders create new strategies or undertake a business transformation:

1. **New leader—new strategy.** The shelf life for a non-founder CEO is about eight to twelve years. CEOs transition due to normal succession planning or lack of performance. In the latter case, if the business is broken or is underperforming, there likely is an urgent need to make strategic adjustments or even transform the business. However, when a new CEO is promoted, or especially if they are brought in from the outside, they typically like to roll out a new strategy. It's rare for a new CEO to continue to pursue the previous leader's strategy. What's interesting about this phenomenon is that the strategy is more a reflection of the individual at the top than the company itself. When viewed through this lens, this is the most precarious rationale for a new strategy and especially a transformation.

It's understandable that a new leader wants to make a mark, but the risk is the attachment of the strategy to the leader and not the connection/association of the strategy to the organization and its mission or purpose.

2. **Product or market stagnation.** There are a number of industries that have reached maturity and will not be around in the future. Some of these companies are able to foresee the trend and proactively adjust their strategy well in advance of the change. And many of these companies are able to make these pivots time and again. For instance, I remember as a kid growing up in the 1970s watching the gasoline lines stretching for blocks. Neighbors could only go to the pumps on certain days based on their license plate number. Back then, experts surmised that by the year 2000, there would be no more crude oil left to be extracted, and thus, there would be no more gasoline. In retrospect, there were a number of strategic miscalculations made and in fact, daily crude oil output in 2020 far surpassed that of the 1970s. This was enabled largely through new oilfield discoveries and new technology to extract oil from the earth that was not possible back then. This illustrates how big oil companies have been busy for decades adjusting their strategies to ensure their survival.

3. **Technology upheaval.** The technology changes that affect some industries have been remarkable. One of the most famous cases of technology annihilation is how Netflix destroyed Blockbuster. Netflix clearly understood what it was setting out to do, but Blockbuster did not appreciate the strategic threat and could not bring itself to disrupt its own business model. Blockbuster failed to realize that it was becoming a corporate zombie. It's interesting to think about the tech-enabled disruptors today in the established or entrenched companies that they are trying to upend. In retrospect, it is easy to see how Netflix put Blockbuster out of business. But how many business leaders are running a Blockbuster equivalent in a different industry? At what point do business leaders recognize the threat or the trend?

The auto industry is a fascinating example of a combination of megatrends coming together. First of all, we will eventually deplete fossil fuels, and the industry as constituted depends on combustible engines. Therefore, all auto executives need to incorporate this fact into their strategic thinking. Second, the technological advances in power storage and batteries are making it possible for electric vehicles to take hold. To be sure, the infrastructure for battery-operated cars requires a substantial investment, which likely will be accomplished through some sort of public-private partnership. Again, leaders of traditional car companies who do not incorporate electric vehicles into their fleet strategy will not be successful long term. Third, the strategy of being number one, two, or three in the market is a lazy strategy. Tesla is not even in the top ten of auto manufacturers, yet it currently has the largest market capitalization, with its next closest competitor, Toyota, at a very distant second.[3] Finally, the rise in popularity of special purpose acquisition companies has made it possible for a number of emerging electric vehicle manufacturers to tap the public equity markets, raising capital and their brand profile. Many of these emerging electric vehicle companies will end up failing or being merged into others. However, some of these companies have a market capitalization that exceeds traditional auto manufacturers and may use that inflated currency to buy a traditional player. The confluence of these strategic considerations in the auto industry will be fascinating to watch.

4. **Existential threat.** The most obvious example of an existential threat was the impact of the global COVID-19 pandemic had on many industries, including retail, travel, and entertainment. Many companies were already stretched on their balance sheets. When markets roll along incrementally, debt-burdened balance sheets do not play a critical role in corporate strategy. However, as we saw in these industries, many companies with stretched balance sheets ended up filing for bankruptcy, despite significant government intervention.

Companies end up with stretched balance sheets for several reasons. For the most part, this happens as a result of heavily capital–intensive industries, leveraged buyouts, recapitalizations, or pursuing an acquisition strategy. Rarely does one see stretched balance sheets from working capital expansion due to profitable organic growth.

Companies in many industry sectors have been forced to make quick decisions to ensure their survival. The difference between companies that have thrived during the pandemic and those that have struggled extend beyond their balance sheets' ability to withstand the shock. Companies that have invested in digital tools and engaged consumers in a digital fashion have been able to weather the storm. For example, companies in the casual or quick-service restaurant industry that have had a digital strategy in place to enable mobile ordering and pick-up already in place, such as Starbucks, Chick-Fil-A, or Chipotle, experienced far less revenue impact than their competitors who didn't have mobile capability. Retailers who were able to quickly enable curbside pickup were able to soften the blow to their top-line revenue.

5. **Shareholder activism.** Shareholder activism is a key driver for many corporate strategy initiatives. Activists advocate for change in many ways. They usually want companies to streamline their operations by divesting what they call non-core brands or divisions. In other cases, activists may advocate for combining assets or divisions with other companies in order to achieve scale. There have been some high-profile activist campaigns over the years. In some cases, the CEOs cater to the activists and address their strategy. On the flip side, there are CEOs like Indra Nooyi at PepsiCo, who have stood firm and have actually used activists to strengthen the resolve and the organizational commitment behind its strategy. Watching Nooyi in interviews defend her strategy at PepsiCo against the activists' attacks was a strong display of her leadership and conviction.

Necessary Ingredients for a Successful Transformation

Companies and their leaders learn from their failures and their successes. Through this lens, we try to learn why transformation projects and strategies fail. However, it is equally as important to understand why they succeed. In our experience working with companies to help them create and execute critical transformations, we identified at least seven key ingredients for success. We note, however, that understanding motives comes into play here as well. Companies and their CEOs have motives to embark on strategic initiatives. Assuming the motives are sound, the following components enable success.

1. **Soundness of strategy.** The first component is the soundness of the strategy itself. There are a number of different methods to build a comprehensive and visionary strategy. It is critical to fully understand the organizational motives and strategic imperatives before embarking on a strategy effort. The methods per se are not as important as the robustness of thought, data, and insights used to formulate the strategy. Great leaders engage Amplifiers in strategy formulation. The strategy needs to incorporate physical, financial, and human assets and resources. Amplifiers will stretch the organization to achieve greater outcomes while shoring up areas of the business that need to be addressed. Clearly articulating the critical elements of the strategy, including the vision, goals, metrics, tactics, and road map, is essential for leaders to establish and communicate to the organization. The leader needs to create enthusiasm throughout the organization to increase the odds that they will actively participate in advancing the company toward its stated goal. This is one area where Amplifiers can play a vital role.

2. **Stakeholder alignment.** Stakeholder alignment on a single vision is a necessary ingredient for success. Incorporating Amplifiers or Amplifier representatives from each of the key stakeholder groups ensures that stakeholder needs are either incorporated

into or addressed in the strategy effort. It's generally impossible for all of the needs of all the stakeholders to be met. Therefore, there is a series of trade-offs, resource allocation, risk analysis, and other machinations required to arrive at the strategic vision. Given these trade-offs, the vision needs to be inclusive enough to paint the picture for those stakeholders who may not benefit as much. In this way, Amplifiers play a particularly important role as change agents. As influencers, they can persuade other followers to see the overall benefits of the trade-offs made so that the sum of the strategy and its benefits outweigh the trade-offs and their costs.

3. **Gap analysis.** Unless the strategy is incremental, all transformation efforts require gap analyses that clearly define organizational shifts that are required to achieve the new vision. This gap analysis typically involves a comprehensive review of the current state of the business. For example, a biopharma company seeking to excel in oncology therapies might realize a gap it has in its R&D pipeline or depth of bench scientists able to discover new oncology drugs. Amplifiers help to increase the impact of gap analyses by critically assessing the strengths and weaknesses of the company to ground the vision in reality, while providing an achievable picture of the future.

4. **Funding the journey.** Executives need to properly allocate financial and human resources to enable the success of the transformation journey. Leaders need to understand the long-term investments required to fully execute the strategy. This inevitably requires a set of trade-offs between short-term projects and, in some cases, conflicting change initiatives. As a result, there is a series of start-stop decisions as well as reallocation of human resources to properly staff the initiative. In the end, the funding needs to support the strategic journey.

5. **Change is communicated and role modeled.** The case for change presented to the organization needs to be compelling and well communicated. Furthermore, the organization needs to see the leader role-model the behavior it expects to change. When

Amplifiers are aligned with the leader, Amplifiers can help communicate and model this change to the broader organization.

6. **Accountable execution.** Most corporate strategy projects involve a series of work streams. Each of these work streams needs to clearly fit together with visible goals, schedules, and allocated resources. Leaders need to be accountable to the organization to execute the strategy work streams, as well as to deliver the promised business benefits. Over the years, we have seen leaders roll out new strategies to be met with skeptical eyes among the rank-and-file employees as they view it as the "strategy du jour." Being accountable along the way, leaders can deliver on elements of the strategy by setting the foundation, building credibility, and gaining momentum throughout the organization.

7. **Agile execution.** Companies are shortening their strategic planning horizons and embracing a more agile strategy execution. Consumer trends, technology advancement, shrinking R&D discovery cycles, and other factors demand that companies rapidly adjust to changing market conditions, many times midstream. Companies who have an agile mindset are not caught up in their own agendas and can pivot more quickly to adjust and capitalize on new opportunities. That said, companies obviously need to understand the difference between short-term adjustments and the long-term strategic impacts of their transformation efforts.

At Clarkston we use an acronym to help the leaders with whom we work succeed in their transformation journeys. We have found that all the elements of EFFFORT need to be incorporated into the strategy or transformation initiative: Energy, Focus, Flexibility, Funding, Organizational (re)alignment, Resources, and Time.

Energy

As mentioned, many new strategies get created when a new CEO is put in charge or if there is a major existential jolt to the company. This seems to be the case whether or not the new CEO is appointed from the outside or promoted from within. Leaders typically want to make their mark on the company, and this is typically done through creating a changed vision for where they want to take the organization. The leadership team sets out with significant energy to frame this new vision, coupled with the drive to push it out throughout the employee base. However, it is amazing how often there is a disconnect between the energy at the top to advocate for change and the inertia present in the organization that is stalled.

In the best of times, a new CEO is appointed after a long, successful career of the predecessor. In this case, the organization is doing well, and the company's flywheel is rotating well without the need to exert much additional energy. This situation presents a challenge for the incoming leader. The organization is accustomed to the success it has generated over the previous years. New strategy and direction may be met with skepticism because the organization doesn't understand why it needs to change its successful methods or why a new vision for the future is even necessary. Here is where the phrase "the good is the enemy of the best" presents a particular challenge for the incoming leader. The new leader needs to channel the positive momentum the company has and frame the future opportunity in a way that will inspire and energize the company into action.

In other cases, the organization is stalled, and the new leader is tasked with changing the course to make new progress. In this case, the leader needs to break several habits throughout the company that are not producing the desired outcomes. Often, companies that are stalled have become complacent or incremental in their thinking and actions. Injecting energy into this environment is essential, albeit complicated. The most effective leaders will tap into Amplifier talent to magnify the impact and create positive energy for this change. In Figure 9.1 we show companies that have overcome the inertia quotient. These are companies that have been established for decades yet continue to innovate their products or how they do business.

Amplifiers create the energy necessary to drive a new strategy or transformation effort. The first activity is to tap into Amplifiers at all

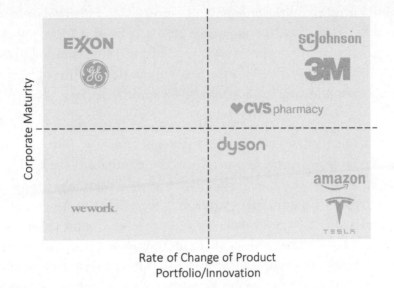

FIGURE 9.1 Corporate Culture: Inertia Quotient

levels in the organization. Without the energy necessary to carry out the change, these projects will fall short of expectations, and thus fail. Amplifiers have a keen sense for the level of energy and effort needed to drive sustainable long-term change, to break bad habits, or to insert positive momentum in other areas.

Flexibility Versus Focus

Any leader who has undertaken a large strategy project or transformation effort understands that rarely do these initiatives go as originally planned. Inevitably something will come up. The world we operate in is not linear. The best laid plans can be disrupted for myriad reasons—internally driven and externally driven. For larger companies, strategies are very complicated and must consider various scenarios, including those with lower probabilities of occurrence. Opportunistic M&A transactions present a common impetus for required adjustments to a strategy. Not all acquisition targets that would be good additions to the portfolio are available for sale at the optimal time. Acquisitive companies understand that when these assets hit the market, the company needs to be able to act quickly. On the flip side, when there is inbound interest for a portfolio asset, leadership also needs to be in a position to act quickly. Long-term portfolio planning needs to be focused and flexible.

Almost all companies are in various stages of executing a multi-year strategic plan. Virtually none of the executives within our client base were able to anticipate the impact the pandemic would have on their ongoing strategic initiatives. Every one of these clients needed to inject flexibility into their strategic plans. Some of our retail clients required wholesale change to adjust to store closures and significant decline in retail traffic. Other clients in our biopharmaceutical practice needed to adjust their focus in the lab to create vaccines and therapies necessary for public health. In other cases, our clients simply needed to make various course corrections to adjust for the virtual work of their white-collar team members while creating the process adjustments necessary to ensure the safety for their frontline blue-collar workforce.

Companies with the vision and foresight to shore up the balance sheet in advance of the pandemic were in a far better position to weather the storm. Many companies learned from the impact of the financial crisis in 2008 and 2009, understanding that they were susceptible to market-driven shocks beyond their control. These companies took action to ensure that their balance sheets were strong so that they could be in a position to make thoughtful decisions without panicking. The pandemic tested the contingency planning element of strategic planning for many businesses. Many strategies are built based on robust market research and projections of demand and competitive positioning. However, downside planning is typically less of a focus. Many times, executives and visionary leaders are optimistic and don't dwell on negative scenarios. Here, Amplifiers are key in playing the devil's advocate role in a constructive and productive manner. The trusted skeptic Amplifier can pose the challenging and critical questions in an effort to shoot holes in the strategy in advance of the strategy deployment. If done well, this prepares the organization to adjust and be flexible when these outside existential shocks hit the market.

However, some organizations fail in part because their strategies lack focus and are too flexible. Although companies need to remain agile, successful companies stay focused on the long-term strategy and do not chase the short-term whims of the next shiny object placed in their path. This is a tricky balance, as we've seen some of the large and established consumer products giants miss major new consumer trends like craft beer or Greek yogurt. So, the balance between focus and flexibility is a fine line that needs to be actively managed.

Funding

One of the essential elements of any transformation effort is the proper allocation of human resources and funding. We are commonly engaged to help leaders create the transformation road map and journey. One of the key elements that drives success is the creation of clear goals and expected business outcomes that are properly funded with a demonstrable return on investment.

Companies make five mistakes when allocating resources for transformation efforts. The first is failing to properly allocate the adequate human resources, internally and externally, to staff the transformation. Another mistake is failing to account for the time necessary to change or influence behavior toward the new destination. This may be because of a lack of appreciation for the current state of the company. Or perhaps the leader has been in an echo chamber and fails to understand the inertia that exists throughout the company.

The third trap is tripping over dollars to pick up pennies. Some pursue quick wins that are worth pennies at the expense of more substantial harder-fought wins to pick up dollars and position the firm in a substantially better place for long-term success. In some turnaround situations, quick wins are necessary to create a stronger income statement or balance sheet necessary for the company to be more strategic in the long run. However, good companies seeking to be great ought to carefully consider the trade-off of pursuing near-certain short-term smaller gains that prevent longer-term and larger gains. Sometimes it is necessary, and more effective, to push for more impactful change, even knowing it may be a harder fight.

The fourth mistake is funding transformations off the company's balance sheet. Some companies justify new initiatives only that are capital projects, leveraged buyouts, changes to revenue recognition methods, or acquisitions that add to goodwill on the balance sheet. Although all of these can be pursued for legitimate reasons, we do see far too frequently how companies get derailed by leaning on these methods instead of building a compelling case with a strong underlying strategic rationale.

The fifth trap is focusing on short-term quarterly performance instead of adequately funding the strategy in the short run to achieve long-term success. There is a disconnect when public companies are taken private because they need to reinvest to transform the business. A notable example is Dell, which was a very successful public company for a period of years but ultimately failed to innovate and needed to transform. Dell was taken private, which enabled it to invest for the long term without the quarterly scrutiny imposed on it by institutional shareholders. I'm always impressed by the CEOs who have the courage to stand up to these institutional shareholders and impress on them that the decisions they are making today will benefit stakeholders years down the road.

Organizational (Re)alignment

Effective leaders understand that they need to have the right organizational structure and culture in order to be successful in carrying out any transformation effort. The right people and mindset are needed to drive change. We have seen time and time again unwillingness from executives to make the changes they know are right.

Great leaders understand, as Jim Collins states in *Good To Great*, that having the right leaders on the bus is essential for long-term success. One of the common mistakes or regrets leaders confessed to me is that they waited too long to make a necessary change in key personnel. Rarely do they say that they made the change too quickly. Having the wrong people in key roles never gets better with time. In fact, having the wrong people in key roles has a negative impact on other followers and Amplifiers, and this erodes the credibility of the leader. Leaders are often loyal to these executives, but the rest of the organization already knows they should be swapped out.

Many companies are incremental thinkers and have an incremental culture. Often seen in large and established public entities, these companies evolve in this manner based on long periods of managing quarterly numbers, while individuals in the organization play the political game safe as they seek their next promotion. It is a cascading crescendo of micro-decisions and incremental moves that create a difficult culture for real change to take root. Most companies do not fully see that they are even in this category. They carry out their businesses quarter in and quarter out. We call them *zombie companies* because they are dead and don't seem to recognize it. Unless these companies get resuscitated, they will not perform better than overall GDP. Many of these companies can change course to become more innovative or entrepreneurial with the proper injection of a combination of long-term thinking, vision, acceptance of failure (experimental, new business model, and innovation failure), and organizational change. Discovering the Amplifiers and potential Amplifiers within these companies can mean the difference between breathing life and energy back into their innovative cores or seeing them wither and fade away into obsolescence.

Over the years, we have seen companies reorganize in an attempt to increase sales or change the culture. Although reorganization can play a role in such change, it cannot be the sole means to the end. It can only be part of the puzzle and not the complete answer. Companies with obsolete product portfolios cannot reorganize their way into success. Companies with static incremental culture cannot reorganize their way into creating a culture of innovation. Leaders pursue reorganizations simply because it is an obvious and public display of "change." However, these leaders are confusing a reorganized corporate hierarchy with the underlying change in mindset that is actually needed for real change to take hold. Amplifiers enable organizational change and mindset change, thus unlocking the power of the masses needed to increase the probability the organization will achieve the strategic goals of the transformation effort. When included as part of a comprehensive strategy, organizational realignments can play a powerful tool for creating lasting change to support the strategy and cultural shifts.

Resources

Adequately resourcing strategic transformation projects is essential. Most companies have more to do than resources with which to do it. Leaders must evaluate the trade-offs and wisely choose between what they are going to do and what they are not going to do. Taking resources away from one area of the business to support another is a difficult decision for many executives to make. Great leaders demand the best people for their transformation efforts. This puts even more pressure on the department managers. Many times, the departments that need to free up resources for a transformation effort often complain that they are already understaffed as it is. But there is no gain without some level of pain. Amplifiers step in to help their colleagues understand the impact in the short run of their increased workload and help the leaders paint the picture for why the change is necessary to create a better long-term and sustainable company for all the stakeholders.

Transformation efforts fail or succeed largely as a result of the people who are assigned to carry out the transformation, but also by the people who need to embrace the work required of the transformed enterprise. Companies with a talent development mindset understand how they need to evaluate and activate Amplifiers to fill critical roles on transformation initiatives. Most large transformation projects require not only identifying outstanding internal resources but also high-quality external resources to support the initiatives. Unfortunately, the purchasing function often plays a more prominent role in selecting external talent than does the HR function. Instead, purchasing should play a supporting role to the HR function when selecting external talent. The HR function has the training and skills necessary to understand the full picture of human talent and culture, enabling the transformation project the best chance for success.

Time

Most transformation efforts worth their weight take time. Patience is a virtue, and effective leaders need to balance making progress with the fact that transformations are multiyear efforts. Organizations require institutional stamina to persevere through these multiyear transformation efforts. This is especially true when the culture needs to be changed, when the change requires long product development cycles, or when the required time to adopt to a particular change is longer than expected. Therefore, leaders need to set achievable interim milestones that have clear goals and expected outcomes. These multiyear transformation efforts are a bit like a relay race. Often, the leader who embarks on the journey and runs the first leg needs to hand the baton to the successor to continue to carry on the race. Amplifiers can help bridge that gap of institutional knowledge and fortitude.

Amplifier Impact on Corporate Strategy

True Amplifiers play a special role in helping companies realize their corporate strategies. Any leader who has undertaken a transformation or strategic initiative understands the crucial role true Amplifiers play. Amplifiers are motivated in a variety of ways to help inform, shape, develop, and execute corporate strategy. These individuals have a special ability to see the future, discern patterns, pick up trends, spot opportunities, and fundamentally see the existential needs to transform. Amplifiers also have a strong sense of responsibility to help the leader navigate the ship into new waters based on a compelling belief in the mission and the purpose of the company. In situations where there is a burning platform, they feel a particular obligation to help the leaders lead the transformation efforts and magnify their power throughout the organization.

Some Amplifiers are motivated by their own personal desires to advance their careers or even by the sense of adventure. Amplifiers are never satisfied with the status quo, and they have a strong sense that any company not advancing forward is actually falling behind. They are not afraid of change and in fact garner energy from change in the desire to constantly improve how they are operating as a company.

Successful companies use Amplifiers to serve as the upward feedback mechanism to advocate for change and bring fresh ideas into the strategic planning process. Given that Amplifiers exist throughout the rank-and-file employee base of the company, their ideas are closer to the action in the field and, if channeled correctly, can bring tremendous insight into the strategic planning process. Because most Amplifiers have a low self-orientation, they place a higher value on the company and its many stakeholders than they do on themselves. The pureness of their motives means the strategic inputs are often synthesized into recommendations that circle back up the corporate hierarchy.

Some leaders are gifted at anticipating the future but are unable to translate that vision into language and actions the organization can understand. The leader may suffer from "Cassondra's Curse"—the blessing of the power to see and predict the future, but the curse of being unable to paint a clear picture of it. Often, such leaders speak in "riddles" when describing the vision and are not fully able to cascade the transformational vision throughout the organization. Amplifiers play a crucial role in translating the vision to a believable course of action for the rest of the organization to follow. They bring a unique blend of closeness to where the rest of the company stands today and an understanding and appreciation of the leader's vision for the future.

In other cases, leaders and their executive teams get excited about a particular idea or strategy. To achieve these goals, these leaders need to be involved in more than just the ideation and the vision but also to oversee the execution. Frequently, and given the demands on their time, some leaders will kick-start the strategy or transformation effort and then get distracted or pulled into other seemingly more pressing or urgent matters. Effective leaders need to balance these inevitable conflicts by strategically delegating when appropriate while publicly supporting the initiative through to completion. Amplifiers can play an important role in enabling the leader not to fall into the trap of believing the "innovator must be the implementer." Amplifiers enable leaders to be part of the execution in a visible way while still maintaining focus on other aspects of the business.

One of the key challenges in executing corporate strategy and especially transformation initiatives is the dual engine dilemma, which suggests that the organization must operate dual engines—the current business and the newly conceived transformed business. In many cases, the new engine cannibalizes the bread-and-butter existing business. In other cases, the new engine requires implementing a business model that contradicts the company's legacy success. Nurturing the new engine while keeping the lights on in the existing engine is not an easy task. Occasionally, inertia will drive energy toward the existing engine, and the organization may consider the new engine a distraction. Here's when Amplifiers can play a critical role in helping the organization power through the dual engine dilemma. They can help leaders communicate the need to reallocate resources toward the new lines of business that do not seem to advance the company's legacy economic engine. In some cases it may be an obvious extension to the product line, and in other cases it may be a revolutionary new model for bringing value to customers. In both cases, Amplifiers are able to articulate the benefits of the new strategy in a way that influences others to join the effort.

Take the auto industry as a classic example of the dual engine dilemma. All of the top ten auto manufacturers are facing the same fundamental strategic considerations. The pace and approach that each considers will be the difference between winners and losers. What will separate the strategies these auto manufacturers will deploy over the next decade will depend largely on their corporate culture and the degree to which they have Amplifiers throughout the organization driving change.

In the case of Volkswagen, we saw how a corrosive corporate culture can destroy consumer confidence and lead to widespread deceit. The top-down nature of their command-and-control hierarchy, coupled with sheep-like followers, yielded poor performance and ineffective strategic decision-making. The issue facing the automakers has been obvious since the oil crisis of the 1970s. Emerging battery technology and the strong consumer desire to eliminate greenhouse gases are market forces now at play that were not as prominent decades ago, when the auto manufacturers were facing the same dual engine dilemma. Until Tesla entered the market, there was no real competitive threat to cause the organizations to move away from their primary economic engine. Great companies, such as Apple, Google, 3M, Amazon, and others, leverage Amplifiers within to spot and act on innovative new opportunities to change their economic engines ahead of it becoming a crisis situation.

There are always more exciting ideas than organizations have the time or resources to pursue. Great companies and their leaders need to make these strategic trade-offs. Trade-off indecisiveness is a crippling handicap for companies and titled executives. Organizations must have a way to effectively and efficiently decide what they will do, what they will not do, and what they will stop doing. Amplifiers are able to magnify the strengths and weaknesses of the strategic choices confronting leaders and help them arrive at the best possible decisions. When organizations add new strategic initiatives and do not make the proper trade-off regarding what they are no longer going to do, the organization feels overburdened. Amplifiers can magnify the voice of the broader employee base so that leaders can appropriately disengage with certain nonstrategic initiatives or initiatives that may conflict with the ability to deliver on the transformation goals.

Nelson Mandela said, "When conditions change, you must change your strategy and your mind. That's not indecisiveness, that's pragmatism."[4] It is important to remain flexible while engaged in a transformation journey, which is long and hard and is never a straight line. The leaders and Amplifiers supporting and enabling the effort must often check progress against success measures, adjusting the course as necessary. They may need to scrap ideas that are no longer relevant or double down when new ideas emerge that are primed for magnified success. It is essential to adjust as conditions change while maintaining focus on the overall transformation journey.

When new CEOs are brought in from the outside, there is a natural period of time necessary for them to earn the trust of the organization. In other cases, as was the case of GE under Immelt, the CEO or titled executive has a high degree of self-orientation and the broader employee base is unsure whether the executive is out for himself or knows what's in the best interest of all the stakeholders. When there is lack of trust, dysfunctional and passive aggressive behaviors permeate the organization. Amplifiers play a critical role in building the trust bridge between executives and the broader employee base when needed. When trust exists, the organization will go to great lengths to help execute the strategy. Companies that operate with a high degree of mutual trust are able to form high-performing cross-functional teams that work together to deliver a common goal. During the inevitable peaks and valleys of the difficult transformation journey, this highly functioning team will be able to deliver a clear vision and strategy, magnified by trust and respect for one another. These high-performing teams remain aligned and focused on the priorities and goals at hand and are especially effective when leveraging the power of three Amplifier concept from chapter 3.

Most transformation efforts will encounter an unforeseen problem or mistake along the way. The best leaders will immediately step up and own the mistake. By publicly praising the individual who pointed out the mistake, the leader helps create a culture in which employees feel comfortable bringing forth shortcomings or defects that can be addressed early on in order to avoid disastrous long-term consequences. It takes a degree of humility for a leader to own the mistake and praise the person who brought it forward. Amplifiers hold their leaders accountable and keep them honest with this practice. They demand excellence and will constantly raise the bar for performance regardless of whether it is the leader or another colleague within the company.

Establishing Trust in the Business Transformation Process

In order to gain trust, one must put oneself in a vulnerable position to establish a rapport of openness and honesty. Regardless of whether things need to change due to internal or external pressures, a leader's job is to articulate the vision and build a team that can navigate change. A team is not a team without trust. Under the added pressure of change, trust is even more critical. This is true in personal and professional relationships.

- Think about how successful your leadership team has been lately. What role has trust played in that success? Have you seen tangible examples where trust was a clear differentiator and/or had a significant impact?
- Think about how deeply rooted trust is within your organization. How do you measure your employees' trust in senior leadership? Regardless of the input, how do you leverage that information to drive business decisions?

- What motivates teams to go above and beyond? Does trust play a role?
- Whose responsibility is it to build trust across the organization/team?
- What steps can you take to build or rebuild trust?

Growth without change is impossible. Trust is essential in leading organizations to change, but especially through the business transformation process.

Meaningful corporate strategies designed to create transformative business results inevitably create varying degrees of friction. Great companies and leaders embrace friction where it counts. Transformation requires the elimination of strongly held business models and paradigms and forces individuals to stretch or abolish the preconceived notions about the business and its goals. A lack of friction and transformation often means that the business isn't actually changing; it's repositioning or shifting but not actively transforming. Embracing the friction ultimately drives a better outcome for the business as a whole. By removing the conflict powered by egoism or fear, the remaining friction empowers business transformation.

Friction forces leaders to reexamine positions, test boundaries, challenge the strategic beliefs. These are all elements of a genuine transformation. As long as leaders are aligned to the ultimate goal and are committed to change, friction serves as a positive means to the goal. Amplifiers bring out creative friction among the key stakeholders to ensure diversity of thought, and differing perspectives are brought to bear not only in the formation of the new strategy, but also in its execution.

10 Amplifying Change Management

True Amplifiers play a critical role in bringing strategy to life. They amplify good change management strategies created by companies and fill in the gaps when companies undertake transformations without sufficient change management support. John Kotter essentially popularized what is known today as change management in the corporate setting.[1] His thinking and concepts were groundbreaking at the time. The trouble is, there has been little advancement of his theory in the past three decades. In fact, there has been as much literature written about why change initiatives fail and an equal amount written regarding why strategy initiatives fail. The world has evolved in several major dimensions since change management was established, yet the thinking has not kept pace. The purpose here is not to reinvent the classical change management thinking but to highlight the ways in which Amplifiers play a key role helping change leadership magnify business results.

The irony is not lost on us that one of the core disciplines of effective corporate execution—change management—has not progressed substantially since the days when John Kotter popularized the discipline. Yet most of these change efforts fail to deliver on their stated benefits. A similar percentage of large mergers or acquisitions also fail to achieve their intended goals. After layering in other large change initiatives, the numbers remain the same. This begs the obvious question: if so many strategic initiatives or transformations fail, why are they pursued by so many corporate executives?

Corporate transformation or strategic initiatives are generally put in motion as a result of corporate strategy formulation. Other initiatives are created as a set of cascading projects related to the customer, product innovation, supply chain, R&D, or other functional or geographic strategies. Change initiatives don't lead strategy formulation; it's the other way around. All business leaders have a responsibility to ensure that the companies they lead are generating returns for shareholders, employees, customers, society, and other stakeholders. Good business leaders, therefore, set about critically assessing their companies and how they interact with their stakeholders while remaining competitive and differentiated. They have a responsibility to do this in the short term as well as the long term. It is because these leaders are constantly trying to improve their competitive position or grow into new markets that they embark on new strategic initiatives.

There are several fundamental reasons why change efforts fail. Any, or all of the following reasons may be responsible for a failed initiative:

1. **The strategy itself is flawed.** The first obvious reason why change efforts fail is that the strategy itself is flawed. Flawed strategy can be developed in many ways. A striking example of flawed strategy is King Vasa's massive battleship. The king had a vision for a battleship with cannons on multiple decks and ordered the shipbuilders to build it. He failed to incorporate the basic physics of buoyancy and the ship was doomed before it sailed out of the Stockholm harbor. This was compounded by the lack of courage his followers had to escalate the issues to him. Another more recent example is seen when examining the remarkable acquisition strategy pursued by Michael Pearson, an ex-McKinsey consultant, at Valeant Pharmaceuticals. It was obvious to most outside observers that the strategy would end

badly. Not only were there the inherent acquisition integration risks but also there was no way he could have gotten enough synergy of the business to sustain the increased debt burden and balance sheet strain.

2. **The strategy is a me-too follower.** Over the years, we have been engaged by some of our larger clients after they have brought in management consultants to create their top-down strategy. It's amazing how often we see some of the same off-the-shelf recommendations repeated. There is some validity to a fast follower approach to strategy formulation. However, an effective strategy should be unique to the company it is intended to serve. Attempting to fit a me-too square strategy into a round peg will not produce the desired results.

3. **The "anti"-preneurial strategy.** Large successful companies have a tendency to miss obvious trends in part because their brands or products are so successful. It's hard for leaders to argue for a change strategy that may potentially cannibalize product market share when the current strategy is already successful. One of my favorite examples is the Greek yogurt market, popularized by Chobani. Hamdi Ulukaya bought an old yogurt processing plant in upstate New York from a major consumer goods company for less than $1 million.[2] From this humble start, he created a $1 billion company and new category of Greek yogurt in the US market. This new entrant completely upended the strategies of established consumer goods giants. These giants completely missed this new growth market because they could not see how their successful yogurt brands could be uprooted by an upstart. This is not a one-off situation. We see it in the craft beer brewers attack on the big brewers, healthy and fresh options available at food retailers, telemedicine upending traditional health care providers, technology-enabled mortgage lending upending traditional banks, and the list goes on. These large well-entrenched companies spent millions on their strategies, yet they were not entrepreneurial and failed to foresee new entrants or substitutions. It is a classic example of how good is the enemy of the best.

4. **Misaligned interests.** Misaligned interests between owners and operators can sink a change management strategy. This has been especially evident in the retail industry. Many retailers have been bought, sold, taken public, taken private, or have otherwise changed hands over the years. The main beneficiaries of these change efforts were the private equity owners who leveraged up the balance sheet in order to juice their returns. This is an effective and common private equity strategy for the owners, but oftentimes, this strategy ends poorly for the company, as was clear when the global COVID-19 pandemic hit. The catastrophic disruption in retail sales forced many retailers ending up in bankruptcy. In nearly all of the cases, the company's balance sheet could not withstand the economic shock caused by the pandemic. The debt amassed by these retailers was not sustainable. This put enormous pressure on the maintenance of steady sales, which is extremely difficult in the retail business as it is and proved impossible for many during a pandemic.

5. **Weak organizational commitment.** One of the key responsibilities that a leader has is to engage the organization and its stakeholders in the transformation journey. When there is a burning platform, it is easier to get stakeholders on board. But a burning platform is rare. More often, the employee base is comfortable operating in its current construct. Comfortable employees have a tendency to resist change. This creates one of the big paradoxical challenges for leaders. On the one hand, they want to create an environment where employees feel safe and don't need to look for other jobs. On the other hand, leaders need to create some angst to push people out of their comfort zone and toward the change necessary for the future competitiveness and sustainability of the company. Strategies are not worth the paper they're printed on if the humans in the company are not willing or able to carry out the necessary changes. Human nature is often change averse. Fortunately, we've seen that true Amplifiers generally advocate for change as early adopters. Good leaders will tap into these true Amplifiers to increase the odds that their strategies will deliver the results expected.

Effective leaders need to set the vision and carry out the mission of the organization. Oftentimes, the organization needs to transform as a result of market changes due to competitive pressure, an existential threat, a technology modernization effort, or supply chain reorganization. In other cases, it may be the result of a merger, acquisition, or corporate reorganization. When these situations arise, leaders rely on true Amplifiers to both carry out the transformation journey, as well as to lead other employees along the way.

One example that highlights how Amplifiers magnify the impact of positive change within companies occurred with early interactions I had with Tim Hassinger, who later became the CEO. Hassinger was an up-and-comer and relatively new in his career. He was assigned to work in the supply chain area, ultimately reporting to Jim Theis. Theis was a hard-nosed and demanding executive. I remember getting particularly nervous when I would need to go meet with him, because he was always a bit skeptical about consultants. He had high expectations and was a highly demanding manager, even more so for consultants. I knew I needed to be on my game when I met with Theis. Fortunately, we both knew that we needed each other in order for us both to deliver what was promised in the joint venture integration. He also knew that I could play a valuable role in the development of his key leadership development candidates.

Theis described his vision for what he expected out of the joint venture and the efficiencies he saw across the supply chain, working capital, and customer service levels. Planning in the seasonal agricultural business is particularly challenging, especially with the technology tools we had at the time. It was in one of my meetings with Theis where he explained how they rotated their high-potential employees through certain roles in the company and that I would benefit from learning from Hassinger, and he would benefit from learning from me. Theis emphasized to me that Hassinger's peers would look to see how he adopted the changes that we were making and if Hassinger was on board, they too would come aboard.

What I've learned over the years working with hundreds of companies and thousands of these change agents is that what was at play was Hassinger's followership skills. He was a true Amplifier, that kind of employee who combines leadership and followership into a single package. Like electricity needs AC and DC current, Amplifiers need leadership and followership current.

Companies have been burned by a highly charismatic leader who has made lofty proclamations or made a highly publicized transformative acquisition, yet the organization failed to deliver on the promised benefits. After the ceremonious firing of the failed CEO, the organization settles back into its safe zone. Companies with this corporate post traumatic stress disorder may be reluctant to initially step forward and follow the direction of the new leader. Some employees will say to themselves, "I will put my head down and do my work as I have done it. This change won't last, the leader will be gone, and all will be back to normal soon."

Change management as a discipline grew out of research and study of human behavior. People don't want to be managed into changing what they do. They want to be led or inspired to do things or act differently in the future rather than conform to a set of behaviors dictated from above. It may seem like a subtle difference, but the power of the transformation lies in the subtlety.

Let's take a look at some common behaviors that lead to a reluctance to change and the barriers that organizational leaders face when influencing people to carry out the stated strategy. Most companies are generally well run and produce good results. As a result, the case for change is significantly more difficult. Employees that try to enact anything more than an incremental change run the risk of taking on significantly more work and/or alienating key internal constituents to accomplish the contemplated change. Early in my tenure at our firm, we were working with a divisional president for one of the leading global cosmetics companies. We outlined elements of a strategy that would bring substantial topline revenue growth while saving significant sales, general, and administrative costs. Although he was appreciative of our work and he committed to pursue some of the strategies put forth, he explained to me that the company's incentive structure centered on incremental gains. The introduction of substantive changes would not be well received. It was a genuine "don't rock the boat" rebuttal. The company was very successful; it was, and still is a "good" company. However, although a clear path to making the division "great" was outlined, the executive could not get on board because the change would disrupt their current comfortable position. This is a clear illustration where good was the enemy of great.

Habits. Conventional wisdom says that bad habits are practically impossible to change. Bad habits are identified through performance reviews; called out by leaders, managers, or even colleagues; but the behavior can be remediated. Bad habits are generally corrected by diagnosing and consciously working to create the corresponding positive habit. Over time and with practice, the behavior can be remedied. However, it's not as obvious when it comes to good habits, which creates a paradox. Good habits exist in individuals as well as in corporations. You might argue that if we possess good habits, why change? When these good habits are producing good results, employees are comfortable and generally rewarded for the behavior. When the leaders see that these behaviors or habits, although good for today, will be insufficient for future competitiveness, they have a responsibility to change good behaviors and make them better. Changing good habits to make them better is far more difficult than changing bad habits to make them good.

One of my favorite examples is the application of data analytics to professional baseball, as I mentioned in the introduction. Major league scouts recruited new ballplayers the same way for one hundred years before Billy Beane and the Oakland Athletics changed the game. What the scouts were doing was good and produced good results in baseball for its first century. What Beane introduced was better. At first, it was very difficult for the major league baseball establishment to accept his new methods. He had the conviction to stick with this strategy and make the changes necessary to accomplish the transformation. Beane was a true Amplifier. He could see the future, had to convince the ownership of the team, his scouting staff, and the manager that his new approach using data analytics would produce championship results. For most leaders, their companies fly under the radar and it's not nearly as public. But the challenges are real, nonetheless.

Benefits. I'm always impressed at the level of effort companies put forth before they undertake a strategic initiative or transformative project to get it approved. This should absolutely be done. But what amazes me is that for all the work companies put in before they embark on these initiatives, they rarely track the benefits back to the original request, and if they do, it is a cursory review. Executives seem more interested in getting the approval to start than actually delivering the intended result. There are of course exceptions to this, usually in organizations where there is substantial consolidation of controlling ownership. We've seen many multiyear transformation efforts outlive the executives that put forth the original approval requests. It can be uncomfortable to be accountable for delivering the promised results as these initiatives get underway. But one of the reasons transformations fail is that the leaders in the broader organization fail to keep the eye on the prize. To be sure, outside factors are constantly changing and the benefits should be agile in order to accommodate the changing market dynamics. But a clearly articulated goal, represented through the business benefits, should be front and center of all transformation efforts.

Episodic versus continuous. One of the things we've noticed is that companies that treat change management as a continuous journey tend to outperform the companies that view change management as an episodic or project-related activity. When the changing behaviors and mindset become part of our daily thought process, the organization is in a much better position to capitalize and adapt. In *On the Origin of Species*, Darwin concluded that the organisms best suited for survival are those that are best able to adapt to change.

The global COVID-19 pandemic clearly highlighted this premise across corporate organisms worldwide.

Here is where change management thinking has not kept up. Leaders embark on a strategic transformation project and set up the change management work stream. Imagine an organization with an active, continuous change mindset, one that embraces change at every turn and is passionate about doing things better or different constantly. Change management work streams associated with any project will be more successful with that cultural mindset already in place. So, the challenge we have is not the change management processes per se, but to change the environment that these projects merge into.

By nature, true Amplifiers invite change. They have the ability to anticipate a better future or way of doing things and they step up and make a difference. Amplifier thinking can be a force multiplier and can prepare the organization to accept change as necessary. Companies that are not moving forward, or changing, are losing their competitive position in the marketplace. Therefore, change is not optional. Change is necessary.

Fear. Fear dominates many aspects of our lives professionally and personally. People are afraid they will lose something they have or not get something they want. The best and most effective leaders are able to empathize with the fear that individuals in the broader company experience. Culture plays a key role in the magnification or diminution of fear within the company. Fear is a major barrier to change. Unless the leader minimizes fear as a motivator, fear can create inaction and perpetuation of the status quo. True Amplifiers work through and conquer fear throughout their careers. Amplifiers have developed a set of tools to help them courageously face their fears so that they can productively accomplish what is in front of them.

Understanding the fears of the executive team, the second-tier teams, and the organization as a whole is a valuable investment. Similar to an inventory, fear is measurable. Understanding the organization's fears will pay dividends, because it will enable the future proofing and personal buy-in of the employee base. Leaders are better able to manage those fears through their messaging and influence if those fears are brought to the forefront.

Fear can drive employees to make disastrous decisions. A good example of this is the fear instilled in Wells Fargo employees if they did not hit their sales quotas. At the core of Wells Fargo CEO John Stumpf's "cross-selling" strategy was encouraging new and active customers to open multiple accounts across its various product offerings. Branch managers would instill significant fear in the ranks by threatening termination if employees did not perform. In addition, because their compensation was so directly tied to hitting these quotas, employees feared they would not earn the bonuses associated with opening new accounts. Employees were under tremendous pressure to hit their new account openings targets, so some ended up by falsifying documents to open unwanted accounts, unbeknownst to the customers. Although there were several employees who spoke out about such unethical and fraudulent practices, they were quickly silenced by Wells Fargo's HR group.

Commitment. Most strategies or transformation efforts take time before the results are known. These initiatives are launched with much fanfare, lofty goals, proclamations, and expectations. Then, the hard work begins. Teams are formed, data are collected, and work streams begin their work. There is usually a period of time when the organization has partial information, and there may even be some frustration raised to managers by employees who are "watching the sausage being made." For companies that have a high tolerance for change in a rapidly evolving environment, this impact is significantly diminished. However, most established companies are more change-averse and this period of a transformation project is critical. The commitment to carry forward with the change necessary can be difficult to sustain. Most transformation efforts will go through difficult patches. One or more of the key stakeholders, whether they are internal or external, will resist some element of the effort. Rarely is it easy for everyone to see the desired outcome through a purely objective viewpoint. True Amplifiers play a particularly important role at this phase of any transformation effort. Amplifiers have the professional will and resilience to carry forward during times when the commitment is wavering throughout the broader employee base.

For research-based companies, some R&D initiatives can take up to a decade or more to bring to market. Years ago, one of my clients analyzed data of a competing product and noticed that natural resistance was beginning to erode the efficacy of the primary competitive product on the market. This competing product had the dominant market share, with the second-leading product lagging significantly far behind. My client's product was behind the second competitor. He realized that over time, due to the natural resistance of the market leader, his product could gain significant market share as a viable substitute. This initiative required heavy investment in time and money as well as a lengthy regulatory approval process. This was not an easy sell for him in the executive suite. However, it was an example of a well-thought-out strategy and the leadership commitment to power through the numerous challenges they faced when their product was still an underdog facing a major competitor.

Vision. Leaders have a way of seeing things before the rest of the organization does. There is an ancient Greek parable describing how the Greeks would put lanterns on their feet to shine light along their paths. They could not see their ultimate destination, but if they kept moving forward, step by step, their lanterns would provide enough light for them to continue to make progress. Leaders see the ultimate destination and have a responsibility to illuminate the path toward it for their followers. Some Amplifiers have the ability to see the destination and join arm-in-arm with the leaders to bring the rest of the company forward. Frequently, leaders needs to encourage their followers simply to take the next step. It's unlikely all of the people in the organization will clearly understand the ultimate vision the leader has, or how to get there. Therefore, leaders and Amplifiers need to create a safe environment and shine light on the organization's next step. They need to keep the lanterns on the shoes illuminated to remove fear and uncertainty from the employees so that progress can continue.

Amplifiers play a special role in helping others see what's ahead of them and to prepare them for the upcoming change. There is no way that a small team of leaders at the top can exert enough influence without leveraging others to help them disseminate the message and act as role models for the change.

Change under crisis. Winston Churchill is commonly credited with saying, "Never let a good crisis go to waste." Despite the significant toll that the global COVID-19 pandemic caused on human lives and economic destruction, I'm hopeful that it will cause a permanent change in how we approach education in America. For various reasons, there has been little innovation in how we educate our young people as well as how we upskill workers for better careers. There has been some experimentation with public school education, but the overall construct has experienced incremental change at best. We are not educating our children in a comprehensive, inclusive way. The pandemic forced us to completely change education, literally overnight. The change to virtual classrooms exposed significant disparities across economic, racial, and social lines. These inequalities need to be corrected in order for us to create an environment in which all will benefit. "The rising tide lifts all boats," as the saying goes. To accomplish this, we need to invest in the underlying infrastructure necessary. We will also need educators and administrators to rethink the possibilities presented in a more interactive and dynamic way in online and off-line educational environments. With an open mindset and the commitment to improve outcomes for all, there is a unique opportunity to change how we have been educating our children for the past one hundred years.

Age and maturity of a company. The age and maturity of a company affects the propensity of the company to change. As we have seen, successful companies often resist change for fear they will lose the good thing that they have. Long-established companies also settle into the rut of their comfort zones. Open highways in the desert form ruts where the tires hit the road in the heat of the sun. Even before cars had automatic sensing devices, they could stay in the lane for long stretches due to these ruts. This is true for companies as well. Companies form routines and processes they repeat without much thought. In some cases, the business reason for a particular process has long since vanished; they continue executing tasks without knowing or questioning why those tasks must be done. It is hard to change or challenge the corporate rut.

Companies at the early stage of their evolution tend to be more of a learning organization. They experiment, fail fast, learn, and grow. However, companies that have been around for a half century or more have a tendency to perpetuate the status quo. Experimenting and failing are not as widely accepted, and the consequences are more punitive. This stifles creativity and fuels the fears people have causing them to settle into a bunker mentality. The good news is that there are a lot of exemplary employees at most of these companies. The better news is that there is a lot more untapped talent waiting to be set free at these companies. When partnered with the right leaders, true Amplifiers have the ability to tap into the source of human talent and can really make a positive difference for the organization.

Challenge to meet the numbers. When executives roll out new strategies, there is significant pressure to succeed, which can strain the organization. Although strong leaders may have audacious goals, they complement those lofty expectations with inspiration and a vision for how to accomplish them. We see in the Volkswagen and the Boeing 737 Max cases how titled executives set forth big strategies along with the pressure to achieve the goals at all costs. The combination of big goals and immense pressure produced fatal results for both. Also, the Volkswagen and Boeing executives lacked Amplifier traits, but the change implications throughout the company and their culture perpetuated the fatal strategy. Amplifiers play an indispensable role when executives roll out a new strategic agenda or transformation effort with an iron fist. Inevitably, things will go wrong as they do with any complex strategic initiative. When the culture suppresses bad news, worse news comes to light down the road.

Amplifiers will speak truth to power and raise unpopular points of view regardless of the consequences. Amplifiers gain energy from leaders, but when the top positions are occupied by titled executives, they pull energy from other Amplifiers in their circle. This works for companies that still have enough Amplifiers among the ranks. Unfortunately, some companies reach a tipping point where they no longer have enough Amplifiers to effect positive change. Therefore, one of the critical activities for any organization is to analyze and track its mix of employees to identify and cull exemplary followers and Amplifiers, not only to track potential leaders.

Changing the Mix

In most companies, there is a mix of Amplifiers, detractors, and those who are indifferent and are along for the ride. We notice that in the highest performing organizations, Amplifiers make up anywhere from 20 to 30 percent of the workforce. Unfortunately, detractors also make up a relatively large portion—up to 20 percent.

In Figure 10.1 we start with the "indifferent" center. This group of employees makes up a large percentage of the majority of most companies and could become either Amplifiers or detractors. This is where investing to get a better understanding and appreciation of the employee base yields benefits. It is impossible for a few leaders to gain this level of insight without help from within. Therefore, cascading this to Amplifiers proves to be a valuable source of leverage. The key to moving people in the indifferent center to amplify the change is to understand where they are and what their motives are. This is virtually impossible to do at scale, but true Amplifiers can determine the elements at play in the indifferent center that can be influenced, thereby obtaining the buy-in, commitment, and engagement of these employees in the change effort. In some cases, it is as simple as paying attention to their wants and needs and channeling

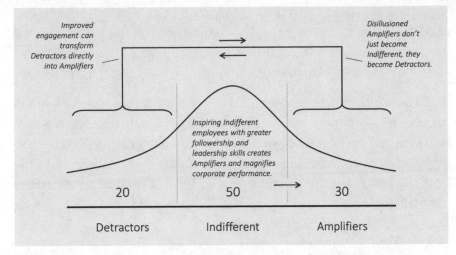

Improved engagement can transform Detractors directly into Amplifiers

Disillusioned Amplifiers don't just become Indifferent, they become Detractors.

Inspiring Indifferent employees with greater followership and leadership skills creates Amplifiers and magnifies corporate performance.

20   50   30

Detractors   Indifferent   Amplifiers

FIGURE 10.1 Creating and Sustaining Amplifiers

those elements of the change journey that best fit. Many people simply want to be told what to do and do not have a particularly strong opinion about how best to get it done. They like clear direction and known goals. Inspiring this category of employee to a higher level of engagement magnifies their production as well as increases the power of the entire team.

Finally, leaders must guard against the indifferent center being swayed by disillusioned detractors. The detractors may be known or obvious, or not. They may be acting on persuasive motives that are not fully aligned with the overall strategy. In all cases, it is critical to understand the impact these motives have on the indifferent center. Because this group in the middle lacks the passion found with Amplifiers or detractors, they are susceptible to leaders with charisma to influence them to sway to the left. Understanding the mix of talent across the spectrum enables leaders to assess the probability that they can influence the middle to move to the right, as well as to contain or eliminate detractors.

Most frequently, neither detractors nor Amplifiers become indifferent. When Amplifiers become disillusioned, they become detractors, assuming they remain in the organization at all. If the leader is able to flip a detractor, they generally become an Amplifier well into the future. This is because Amplifiers and detractors possess both passion and leadership capabilities. It's hard for leaders to be indifferent.

So why do leaders lose Amplifiers as their followers? Amplifiers need to know that the leaders they follow genuinely care about them. We illustrated this previously with the trust equation. When leaders break trust with Amplifiers, these individuals lose confidence in the leader. Trust is hard to earn and easy to lose. Great leaders recognize that trust is built up over thousands of micro-interactions and can be lost with one or two negative actions.

Generally speaking, leaders, Amplifiers, and detractors all have relatively high confidence. This confidence is necessary for the individual to step up and take chances. Confidence is also a source of power that leaders can tap into when engaging a detractor. Because detractors are highly capable and generally influential in the organization in their own right, they will respond well to the personal attention bestowed on them by the leader. Simple acts and genuine follow-through by a leader with the detractor can be enough to get them on board. It's also important to understand why detractors are detractors. Some seem to have been born cynical. They are cynical professionally and personally. Effective leaders must work hard to win these individuals over.

Another common reason that an employee may be an alienated follower is that they were burned previously in their career. They may still be stinging from an experience with a former boss. Or they may have come from a different part of the organization, have been acquired through an acquisition, or have found themselves stuck in their role. Alienated followers may have a chip on their shoulder or hold a certain grudge or, more frequently, have a blind spot that they need to uncover. Completing a reset of their current professional assets and liabilities helps to refresh their perspective and start anew. The best resets are guided through a combination of honest and thorough self-assessment and reviews from peers, mentors, managers, and outside advisors. This information can be critical inputs for mapping out a path for alienated followers as they renew their careers. Amplifiers can partner with these individuals to help them change because Amplifiers refresh their careers frequently.

Finally, detractors may genuinely disagree with the proposed direction or strategy. This is the easiest group of alienated followers to convert to Amplifiers. The trick is getting them to tell you the truth in real time, not just telling you what you want to hear because you are the leader/boss. This is best done in small work groups or one-on-one settings. Although converting detractors may take time and effort, leaders will see the return on this investment through the success of the change effort.

The danger with engaging Amplifiers as the core team to drive change initiatives and key change agents is that others in the organization may dismiss them as being "always on board." Recall that pragmatist followers will ultimately ensure that any transformation effort is successful. This middle group will be watching to see how safe it is to step out and follow the lead. The mere fact that Amplifiers are on board with the change does not provide safety for the passive followers and pragmatist followers. Of course, the conformist followers will come along for the ride in any event.

In most cases, true Amplifiers will have been active in developing the strategy informing the new direction the organization will take. As a result, Amplifiers are generally already on board with the vision for change. Some leaders instead choose to look at the detractors. Detractors are either the biggest problem or the biggest asset for the leader when executing their transformation strategy. If and when detractors come on board, they can significantly effect change for the overall organization. Most detractors are alienated followers who possess independent and critical thinking skills. The broader organization clearly takes notice when a leader switches a detractor to an Amplifier.

It is essential for leaders to deal with detractors quickly in any transformation effort. Leaders can do this en masse by articulating the new strategic direction or cultural shift the organization needs to take in order to compete and win. One of my clients was an organization that had a culture of being super nice and a great place to work, but it was falling behind competitively. The leader needed to change strategy to be more edgy and assertive. The recently promoted leader had been with the organization for decades prior to his ascension to the top. He identified a small group of people that he felt represented the culture away from which he was trying to migrate the organization. One of his internal benchmarks was to gauge how many of them would still be with the organization after a specified period of time. As they migrated the culture to be more assertive, nearly 90 percent of these individuals self-selected and exited the company. This is an objective data point that cultural migration was taking root.

Amplifiers regard strategic change as a leadership challenge and not as a management activity. Companies that take this perspective garner far greater results. Changing how companies perform throughout their entire depth is necessary for any transformation effort. When people are led effectively, results come to fruition. When true Amplifiers are engaged in change initiatives, extraordinary results come to pass.

Performance management at many companies has evolved over time, yet many companies do not fully understand the inner nature of their employees. Many recent innovations in performance management have focused on reciprocal feedback, separating performance and compensation, more real-time and direct feedback, and simplification. Whereas these improvements are beneficial, they do not uncover the most valuable employees. Unless the performance review process uncovers the strong performers *and* strong followers, the organization cannot find its true Amplifiers and ultimately will suboptimize its potential.

We evaluated the elements of change when Amplifiers magnify the impact to turn up the volume on positive change. These range from low-level activity changes through higher-level sustainable influence of thought and behavior. The elements of change we reviewed included tasks, behaviors, styles, inclusiveness of thoughts and ideas, motives, mindset, and culture.

Tasks

Most global companies create robust change management and training plans for minor and major initiatives. The methodology to identify and map for employees the changes required to migrate from the current way of doing business to the future state is pretty well established. Identifying and developing training procedures and courses to help employees change the tasks and activities performed within a particular business process and/or new technology is commonplace. As employees are becoming increasingly familiar with technology advancements, this is less of a challenge but critical to have in place, nonetheless. How employees execute tasks provides a baseline level of expectations of how the employees in the group need to perform their tasks. Some organizations have allowed more latitude for the culture to accept pushback on these new methods. Effective managers work with the change team early on to best understand how the changes will affect their teams and communicate the how and why of the change throughout the process. Doing this effectively will lessen the noise as the team begins to carry out its function using the new methods.

Amplifiers understand that it's basic human nature to resist change. Resistance to change is especially present in large established companies that have been doing business the same way for years. Because Amplifiers are at all levels of the organization, they step in to support their peers and managers to implement the necessary changes. They do this through a combination of learning the new methods and being an early adopter, leading by example, listening to and teaching their colleagues, and effectively communicating upward to their managers and to the engagement team sponsoring the change initiative.

Behaviors

Company performance is driven in part by the sum total of the behaviors demonstrated among its employees. To achieve excellence and gain a competitive advantage, companies need to evaluate the different behaviors that are common among their workforce so that they can encourage the positive behaviors and eliminate negative behaviors. For example, some companies have a culture of deference. Showing deference to superiors or those with more experience isn't necessarily a bad thing. However, the culture also needs to enable fresh perspectives and newness of thought to permeate through established ways of doing business. Companies that squash these ideas need to modify the behaviors of their seasoned professionals to allow for challenges and new thought to bubble up from below. Simultaneously, it is important to change the behavior of the submissive subordinates to give them more followership skills to empower them to challenge up the organization. Companies commonly want to be more innovative, yet they have little tolerance for failure or mistakes. The most innovative companies are constantly experimenting and trying new things. Inevitably, many of these experiments will fail. The most innovative companies celebrate successes *and* failures, because each failure is an opportunity to learn and advance closer to the next success.

Because Amplifiers are lifelong learners, they are students of the kinds of behaviors that necessarily move the organization forward. They are demanding and expect constant improvement. Constant improvement requires exercising the muscles of the different behaviors in order to improve them and create better organizational habits.

Styles

Working styles vary widely among different employees at any company. In some cases, employees are very independent and are perfectly content working in their silo ticking off action items on their list. Others are supportive of and collaborative with their colleagues.

Work style depends on whether or not the employee is a leader, boss, follower, subordinate, or Amplifier. There are a number of basic human traits that affect the style that employees bring to work on a daily basis. Whereas the work style generally remains consistent over time, it may be affected by external events or by employees' personal issues. We saw various examples of this during 2020. The racial justice riots, the pandemic, the virtual work environment, the economic destruction of several industries all contributed to employees' evolving work styles because of fear, anger, frustration, isolation, and a sense of being overwhelmed.

Amplifiers are keenly aware of their colleagues in the work environment. They sense the changes often in advance of the manager of the group and will step in to support their colleagues. Amplifiers understand when to flex their styles and help others to flex their styles on a situational basis.

Inclusiveness of Thoughts and Ideas

Many companies are severely lacking valuable ideas and perspectives because they have not figured out how to tap more inclusive and diverse talent. They rely on the same group of individuals to carry out the major initiatives and lead major groups or functions. They fail to realize that the scope of talent is far broader than the few who are repeatedly tapped for the big projects or high-profile assignments. The most effective companies have figured out a way to create an inclusive environment in which a robust set of thoughts and ideas are captured, shared, and analyzed. When employees recognize that the organization genuinely cares about and actively solicits a wide range of thoughts and ideas, and synthesizes this input into their strategy and culture, they become significantly more engaged and thus improve the impact on corporate performance.

A relentless pursuit of excellence and constant improvement drives Amplifiers to fully explore all the diverse thoughts and ideas in a comprehensive manner so that they leave no stone unturned. The quest of lifelong learners necessarily drives a curiosity to understand various perspectives and incorporate them into their work. Because Amplifiers generally have a low self-orientation, they earn the trust and respect of a diverse set of constituents. They are comfortable putting themselves in uncomfortable situations, because they realize that by being uncomfortable the best learning occurs.

Motives

Understanding the motives of employees within the company is critical if real change is to occur. Different employees are motivated by different factors at different stages in their careers. For example, some may be motivated by career advancement, the higher purpose or mission of the company, recognition for an achievement, money, work/life balance, and so on. Many managers fail to appreciate their team members' motives. These managers attempt to apply a single management style across a team whose members may be motivated in very different ways. We've seen companies with a culture motivated by the accumulation of money or monetary rewards create bad behavior and questionable business practices. On the flip side, good sales managers appreciate the use of monetary rewards for motivating salespeople to hit sales quotas.

Amplifiers take the time to invest in learning how their colleagues are motivated. This includes their superiors, followers, and other peers in the company. By understanding these motives, Amplifiers are better able to frame strategy and activate their colleagues' talents in a way that best aligns to achieving superior results. Amplifiers also have the courage to address bad behaviors driven by unintended consequences of particular decisions or policies created to align with certain motives.

Mindset

Carol Dweck wrote a book called *Mindset* years ago that describes how people tend to develop a particular point of view over time which strengthens and becomes fixed. Unless they recognize and invest in keeping that mindset fresh, they run the risk of creating a fixed mindset. Growth mindsets are the fuel for individual and corporate success.[3] The best companies have incorporated learning and growth into their ongoing transformation journey and daily operations. They are particularly astute at identifying roadblocks or barriers that will narrow learning or solidify their employees in a rut.

Amplifiers have a growth mindset. They use this attribute to help stretch their teams and push the envelope so that the company achieves greater results. Some of the most visible changes we see throughout major corporations are occurring because of the collective growth mindsets of their Amplifiers. These Amplifiers are stretching companies to change employment practices, focus on the environment, appreciate all stakeholder value not just shareholders, integrate work and life, give back to communities, and other things that were seemingly out of scope for companies in their fixed mindsets of decades ago. Breaking down fixed mindsets during transformation initiatives is essential to help lead the organization through the change. There may be pockets of the workforce that cannot see how the organization can transform from the old way of doing things to the new way. Amplifiers lead by example by influencing their colleagues with the fixed negative mindsets, showing them the path forward toward positive change.

Culture

The culture of the company is the most important asset any company has, yet it is not included on the corporate balance sheet. Companies with a toxic culture will inevitably falter, causing loss of jobs and shareholder value. Companies can have a superior strategy but lack the culture and stamina to bring that strategy to fruition.

Building an effective corporate culture takes time; it is not an overnight process. Amplifiers are leaders in creating the long-term and sustainable culture necessary for the company's success. They possess the leadership skills necessary to demonstrate the cultural values through their actions and serve as surrogates for the leaders in their absence. They have the ability to teach and lead their followers not only to do their jobs more effectively but also to be stewards of the culture, behaviors, and styles necessary for the organization to flourish.

11 Amplifying Corporate Racial Justice

The killing of George Floyd by law enforcement kicked off a series of protests demanding societal change. His death was yet another tragedy resulting from racial injustice. Protesters from all walks of life took to the streets demanding change. The time is now for Amplifiers to enact positive change in measurable outcomes for corporate racial justice. We are seeing individual and corporate Amplifiers step forward with innovative solutions to address some of the underlying challenges. John Hope Bryant, founder of Operation HOPE, said to me recently, "Never let a good crisis go to waste." He has partnered with the visionary leader and Amplifier CEO of Delta Airlines, Ed Bastian, to create the HOPE Inside the Workplace Program for Delta employees across the nation.[1] This is an example of a company investing beyond the platitudes in a press release and committing time and resources to genuinely help improve financial literacy and provide coaching to their employees.

I met Bryant at a family wedding in 2010. Bryant describes Operation HOPE as a nonprofit and for-purpose organization working to disrupt poverty. He was inspired to found Operation HOPE back in 1992 in Los Angeles where he shared his vision for the city emerging from the ashes of the Rodney King riots. It was a tall order. Bryant had no experience starting a company, nor were there any example companies of the kind Bryant was seeking to create.

A few years later, I was asked to speak at one of his HOPE Global Forums conventions. This was a great opportunity to support the Operation HOPE mission. On the evening prior to the event, I attended a private reception for speakers and had the opportunity to meet and spend time with one of Bryant's longtime mentors, Ambassador Andrew Young. Young himself is an amazing man. What he endured on behalf of millions of Black Americans who would come after him is a true inspiration. It was interesting to see the interchange between Bryant and Young. It seemed to me that Young took Bryant under his wing to some degree, helping him be a more effective leader, gain more support, and be a better person. Bryant in turn had a lot of deference for Young. It's in the interaction between Bryant and Young where I could see Bryant's followership skills at play.

For years, Bryant has advocated for low-income citizens to improve their financial literacy and economic position in society. Bryant believes in the American dream. He believes that it is open to all Americans, but action is required in order for us to create an environment where it is truly capitalism for all. At the core of Bryant's belief is that we need to help these Americans with a hand up, not a handout.

In his recent book, *Up from Nothing: The Untold Story of How We All Succeed*, Bryant outlines the five key pillars of success: (1) massive education, (2) understanding the numbers, (3) family structure and resiliency, (4) self-esteem and confidence, and (5) role models. Bryant uses his own life experience to unpack these five pillars and demonstrates how they are in fact available to all. Remember these pillars are coming from the man who founded Operation HOPE after the Rodney King riots. He is intimately aware of the disparities and racial injustices presented to Americans based on their race, economic status, connections, educational background, and the like. Yet despite this knowledge, Bryant is incredibly optimistic that economic opportunities are in fact available to all.

One of Bryant's greatest assets is his optimism. He has been fortunate over the years to have been introduced and networked with very influential people. He has been able to amplify these relationships to increase the power of his organization and turn up the volume of change in many parts of the world. Some of these influencers include former presidents, including George H. W. Bush, George W. Bush, and Bill Clinton, as well as countless world leaders, business leaders, civil rights leaders, and other politicians. You can see Bryant's influence in these leaders; he has the ability not only to let them help Operation HOPE but also allow him to influence these leaders to create better and more comprehensive policy or build better businesses with a higher purpose.

Amplifiers within companies inspire allyship among their colleagues to effect change and improve the consistent and equitable career experiences for all. When titled executives are hesitant, their Amplifier employees are leading up and demanding that they incorporate inclusive strategies. There is a sincere desire for companies to improve, yet they have historically struggled to find the right approach. Growing appreciation with corresponding and sustainable action needs to occur at all levels and across all organizations. Specifically, change is needed in the following areas:

1. Criminal justice reform
2. Health care and health policy
3. Education reform
4. Economic security
5. Corporate racial justice

The challenge is extraordinary, yet the benefits are beyond measure. More and more, we are seeing leaders and followers advocate for change issue calls to action. We are seeing business leaders across the nation step up to answer his call. Similar to the video of the lone nut, we are starting to see numerous leaders and first followers take the lead in their respective industries. In order for us to create the actual change necessary, we need to continue to make the work environment safe for more followers to engage in the positive change. As Bryant says, "The urgent always crowds out the important. And business leaders need to work on this important work."

This is where leaders depend on Amplifiers to motivate other followers to take action. Amplifiers have the courage to speak truth to power and they come from the genuine intent of the trusted skeptic. As a result, leaders can rely on them and their advice to help them change the course and culture of the company toward greater corporate racial justice. Amplifiers bridge the gap, simultaneously guiding their leaders while bringing their followers forward. It is through this critical role of the liaison that true change can take root.

Many leadership and management development programs within corporate America do not effectively incorporate racial differences into their methods. Race plays a critical role in the evolution of corporate performance. The ugly truth is that widespread discrimination and bias has negatively affected the advancement of people of color. Systemic racism is a critical issue that needs to be addressed. The protests in 2020 that occurred after the killing of George Floyd set in motion the seeds of change within corporate America. Creating a more equitable corporate racial justice model is one important dimension necessary to eliminate and extinguish the flame of inequality. Bryant encourages companies to stretch out of their comfort zones to explore new boundaries of their thinking. He encourages development programs to be curious—"noisy" as he calls it.

Economic security is one of the critical elements for racial justice. Economic security starts with a good job. Good jobs start with a good education or job training. A good education starts with positive role models and access. As discussed in chapter 5, one of the portfolio companies we are helping to build is Momentum Learning, which has partnered with Morehouse College to create one of the first code schools at a historically Black college or university (HBCU) through its program Momentum@Morehouse. This was an eye-opening experience for me as we learned firsthand how hard it is for students of color to get access to funds to help pay for their education.

The competition for diverse talent is accelerating, especially in the technology field. This is welcome news because technology jobs typically are well-paying jobs. But the challenge we have is creating new sources of talent; that is exactly what Momentum@Morehouse is seeking to solve. This program is designed to transform the careers of its students by teaching them the skills needed to secure a high-paying tech job.[2] We have immediate results from this effort, as some of the graduates have doubled their incomes. But there is more work to do. In order for the program to ultimately reach its success, we need to create better tuition assistance for the students on the inbound side and employer assistance on the outbound placement side for the graduates. Momentum@Morehouse is approaching this challenge in an integrated way by looking at the total talent supply chain from student admissions, education, placement, and career advancement to create sustainable change and true economic advancement for the students they serve.

The next few years will be a true test to see if companies follow through and demonstrate their commitment to sustainable corporate racial justice. In mid-2020, many companies came forward with lofty press releases claiming all they would do to fight for the cause. In some cases, these companies tapped their marketing budgets in order to bolster their image with these messages of enlightenment. But great companies will devote *true investment* dollars that will have a direct correlation to outcomes. Black Americans are watching. Effective leaders are creating the space and empowering Black Amplifiers to help them be better leaders. The average age of an S&P 500 company is now less than twenty years, while the Fortune 500 is much older. There is inherent bias in hiring, development, promotion, and advancement policies in most, if not all, companies. Organizations must adapt their culture in order to create meaningful change in their inherently biased systems. Over the last decade, we've seen great progress elevating the role of a leader overseeing diversity equity and inclusion into the executive suite.

Developing Black leaders and Amplifiers requires a different understanding and approach than developing their White colleagues. The statistics show there are far fewer Black leaders in executive positions at virtually all Fortune 1000 companies. These leaders have had few, if any, mentors of color during their careers, which puts them at a disadvantage. Being mentored by others is a common and effective way to be developed as a future leader. If you're a leader of a team, refer to the list of the top ten to twenty people who influenced your leadership development and the top ten to twenty people you believe you are influencing. Most White leaders I've encountered over the years have admitted to me that their list is too homogeneous. Herein lies the wasted opportunity to cast a wider net in order to develop the best possible talent in a more diverse fashion. One commitment leaders can make is to ensure that their list of mentees has the appropriate mix of racial, ethnic, and gender diversity.

Acknowledging the perspectives young Black professionals bring to the work environment is essential in helping critical processes run effectively. According to former governor of Massachusetts Deval Patrick, leadership by Black people or people from multiracial backgrounds is a bit trickier. He highlights humility as one of the key necessities but emphasizes that is not just because of race. He recalled private conversations about how Black colleagues would be treated differently if they pounded on the table, that some would react with fear and danger. Another item Patrick highlighted as a difference for Black professionals is an acute awareness that there may be skepticism from some colleagues due to their conscious or unconscious bias. That some organizations may have a sort of tissue rejection as Black executives start to fill the ranks. He recalled how it was critical for him to understand that his audience may be skeptical and offered advice to leaders mentoring these young Black professionals. He encourages them to acknowledge that they understand the skepticism and fear and provide strategies to help them work through any issues should they arise. It is exactly the sort of unconscious bias that we need to uncover, discover, communicate, and work to eliminate from the workplace.

Clarkston leadership has spent the past decade working on diversity, equity, and inclusion initiatives, making significant progress in certain areas, especially the advancement of women to leadership positions. However, despite increasing the size of our Black population within the firm, we were disappointed with their advancement to leadership positions—*and so were they*. I'm grateful that we have a culture where this critical group of stewards felt that they could call us out and confront us with the brutal facts. A few years ago, two of my top partners and I traveled to our Atlanta office for a candid conversation with our Black Steward Network. During this meeting, they freely shared their perspective and helped us understand through numerous examples where we missed the point. One example related to why some of our Black stewards didn't seem to engage with an internal leadership development program we run within our firm. During the course of the year-long program, one of our modules includes studying the Battle of Gettysburg to explore certain aspects of leadership and followership styles. Through these critical conversations, we learned some of our Black stewards were turned off to the program and didn't even want to apply because of the systemic racism and catastrophic oppression the Civil War symbolizes. This information was critical: we were able to immediately pivot and change the program to study the same leadership and followership traits using NASA instead of the Battle of Gettysburg. We can achieve the same teaching environment and skill development in either setting but our new venue is more inclusive, more culturally sensitive, and casts a wider net. We've made other changes as a result of that session and subsequent sessions held with our Black Steward Network.

Actions Leaders and Amplifiers Can Take to Advance Corporate Racial Justice

Years ago, I was working with a leading beauty products company developing their future strategy. One of their strategic objectives was to increase market share among Hispanic and Latino consumers. In a meeting with the president and head of HR, we pointed out that the company did not have proportionate representation of Hispanic and Latino management throughout the company and that if they were genuinely interested in that market, they should create an element of the strategy to address that challenge from within. Our client struggled to see the connection and thus, not surprisingly, fell short of increasing market share in that segment. Leaders in organizations are responsible and accountable to create an environment that is diverse, equitable, and inclusive. Most organizations have a long way to go to achieve this baseline objective. So where do we start to make the change necessary to affect the outcomes required? We have invested time and energy into understanding the steps required and how companies can make these changes.

The first step in the journey to improve diversity, equity, and inclusion within your company is to understand the facts. This starts with analyzing your employee census to look for representation by level, group, and function and comparing that information with the general population and, if possible, with competitors. Once this information is gathered, capturing promotion and advancement rate, salary comparisons, assignments (including assignments on strategic company transformation initiatives), and turnover data creates the baseline from which to set goals. Many leading companies have an objective third-party employee engagement survey, the results of which can be analyzed by race. Understanding differences along racial lines is critical. The emergence of artificial intelligence and other technology tools pointed at this information can yield very interesting and actionable results. Finally, understanding information from exit interviews and job offer rejection interviews may shine a light on racial inequity or cultural biases, especially if you ask the right questions.

Once the data are collected action can begin, and many times action must start where you are standing. As Arthur Ashe said, "Start where you are. Use what you have. Do as you can." We have created a ten-point plan to help companies to create a road map to incorporate corporate racial justice within their company. Figure 11.1 shows the critical elements of a comprehensive view of talent development to advance racial justice within your company.

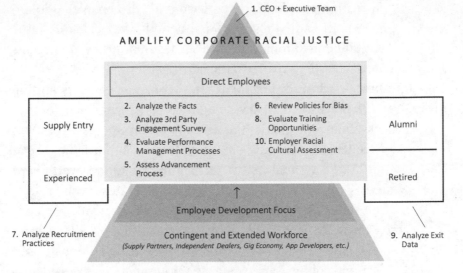

FIGURE 11.1 Amplify Corporate Racial Justice

1. **Let's start at the top.** In 2020, there were eight CEOs of Fortune 500 companies that identified as Black.[3] Of those companies, only a fraction had proportional representation on the executive team, and most had equally low representation on the board. The first challenge to leaders today is to evaluate the team at the top including the succession plans to fill those spots. For most companies, this is an eye-opening task and a difficult pill to swallow. But the truth is we've not done enough to advance Black leadership to the top spots. We've not even done enough to advance Black leadership *into consideration* for the top spots.

2. **Analyze the facts.** Looking at employee census data can be revealing. Much like in Lewis's book, *Moneyball*, companies can drill down into different data points within their organization to truly understand the systemic issues behind the lack of advancement and diversity at the top. At a minimum, the company should collect the following basic data:

   a. Demographic data across key areas such as level or position, function or department, geographic region, and so on. This information should be juxtaposed with the broader population census and if possible, competitive data. This baseline data can be used to understand the future journey the organization needs to strive to achieve.

b. Promotion and advancement rates with a clear understanding of differences across key categories or advancement bottlenecks. Some companies create one or more specific roles that are feeder roles for their emerging leaders. If that's the case at your company, analyze this critical role with an eye toward succession planning and the feeder candidates for the role.

c. Team selection to determine how diverse candidates are chosen to participate in key teams, transformation efforts, and so on. Track the power of three through team composition.

d. Salary and compensation data are important to collect and analyze across the key categories listed in (a). This information needs to be normalized across years of experience and can be easily compared across ethnic and gender differences as well.

e. Turnover data is another key set of baseline information that should be readily available. Understanding turnover by the numbers should reveal information in and of itself. However, companies that dig deeper and try to capture the data points garnered by those who leave will get greater insight into actionable steps to retain talent. For example, a company may find that a particular manager has a disproportionate number of minority employees whose employment is terminated, either voluntarily or involuntarily.

f. Review applicant data for both entry-level and experienced open-hire positions. If the number of diverse applicants approximates the general population, or your company's population, that alone will be revealing.

3. **Thoroughly analyze an objective third-party employee engagement survey and related data.** The construction of the survey also needs to be critiqued in order to understand whether or not it has implicit or unconscious bias. Understanding differences along ethnic or gender lines can reveal opportunities

of strength or improvement. Effectively written and executed employee engagement surveys can uncover a limitless amount of valuable insight.

4. **Evaluate performance management tools, templates, and processes with a particular eye toward ferreting out bias.** Corporate America is littered with performance review templates that are filled with subjective and biased criteria. One example is assertiveness. During a session we had with our Black Steward Network in Atlanta, one of our emerging young professionals shared with us that when he demonstrates assertiveness, people view him as "an angry Black man." As a result, we have better learned to appreciate our biases and he's learned to exert his assertiveness through influence. Our performance review criteria did not account for this racial nuance stemming from others' unconscious biases or unjust stereotypes, because actions are the same for all races but perceived differently due to bias. Reviewing performance management processes for bias is essential, albeit large in scope, for equality in performance ratings, which are essential for equitable career advancement.

5. **Conduct an assessment on promotion criteria, promotion processes, and succession planning and feeder group management.** Understanding bias in the promotion management and feeder group development is essential. Advancement rates are dependent on the development of professionals and how those professionals are mentored so that they are promotion ready. The organization should then peel into the leaders and the diversity of the people they are mentoring. Most companies limit this to teams at the top, but this should be done throughout all levels of the organization. If companies genuinely want to change the color at the top, they need to invest in succession planning in these feeder groups to ensure that Black employees have the mentorship, opportunities, and professional development care and development necessary for them to succeed.

6. **Review written policies and unwritten procedures for bias.** Most companies have an employee handbook that outlines the

organization's policies and procedures. We reviewed scores of these handbooks and virtually all of them need edits to eliminate bias and be more inclusive. There are hundreds of policies, whether written or not, that can be analyzed for bias. Some of these policies are obvious, such as a policy on insuring domestic partners, but many are far more subtle, such as the acceptance of male employees wearing earrings or nail polish. Corporate America is continuing to evolve and be more accepting of individuals from all walks of life, yet its written policies and unwritten practices are not keeping up.

7. **Analyze recruitment practices and data.** One of the critical elements of enhancing corporate racial justice is to analyze the inbound supply of talent. This includes entry level as well as experienced hires. Activating employee referrals is a key way to determine the level of employee engagement. Highly engaged employees tend to refer colleagues to new positions at a higher rate than disengaged employees. Tracking referral rates by ethnicity or gender can be revealing.

   Many highly respected companies are realizing that some of the barriers they have put in place have kept them from evaluating qualified candidates or potential candidates. Capturing applicant data, offer rates, acceptance rates, and other basic information is just the beginning. Many diverse applicants opt out before they even apply based on language in a job description, images on a job board, or the reputation of the company. Once a diverse candidate has made it through the applicant status, they may then opt out due to the lack of diversity of the recruiters or interviewing team. Leading companies who are committed to diversifying their hiring practices are taking the following actions with respect to their inbound recruiting and talent acquisition teams:

   a. They are reevaluating the criteria that set up barriers for diverse applicants. This includes requiring certain levels of education or degrees for certain positions. There are some high-profile executives who never completed their undergraduate education. More commonly, there are tens of thousands of technology developers or application support specialists who have professional credentials or have successfully passed code school certifications, but do not have a four-year degree and are highly capable developers. Companies who require a four-year degree for technology jobs are eliminating a whole group of potentially qualified candidates. Another barrier common for companies and that may eliminate potential applicants is the presence of a criminal record. Companies need to take a fresh look at compassionate policies that enable fresh starts for people. A similar barrier is the historical use of credit reports in the hiring process. There are many low-income families who do not have access to credit and do not effectively build up credit, or their credit is damaged without sufficient resources to correct it. This prevents entire populations of people access to jobs.

b. Once the criteria are established, the job description itself needs to be reviewed. There is new software that will evaluate job postings for unconscious bias. Still more can be done to ensure that the job posting is even more inclusive. It is in the company's best interest to ensure that the net is cast wide so the most qualified candidates come forth. Developing an inclusive job description can help achieve greater diversity of applicants and ultimately hires.

c. More and more, companies are scrutinizing their recruitment pools to ensure they are targeting the most qualified and diverse candidates. For entry-level recruiting, many companies are broadening their reach and expanding to more colleges or different job fairs. For our college recruiting strategy, I assumed that the universities themselves were recruiting a diverse set of students. However, when the actual numbers were pointed out to me, it was clear that my logic was flawed, and we needed to do more to cast a wider net. Talent acquisition leaders need to take direct ownership of sourcing diverse talent and not rely on third-party institutions.

d. Another step recruiters can take to ensure unconscious bias does not affect an applicant is to consider removing names, pronouns, and photos from the résumés and job applications.

e. For the interviews themselves, there are strategies companies are taking to ensure consistency of the interviews and consistent evaluations of the candidates and their responses. Some companies have tests or other qualifying benchmarks during the process, and these qualification exercises should also be reviewed for racial bias. In addition, the interview teams themselves are being trained to eliminate racial bias while interviewing candidates. Finally, many companies are ensuring that their interview teams are diverse.

f. The selection criteria on which the candidates are judged needs to be applied in a consistent and equitable fashion. The more objective the criteria, the more integrity the process will have. Selection criteria, like cultural fit, are critically important, but fraught with racial bias. "Are they a good fit?" takes on an entirely different meaning when considering the impact this question has on minority candidates. Leading companies need to objectively review these criteria and ensure that unconscious bias is not present in either the criteria or how the criteria is applied to candidates.

g. Offer rates and candidate rejection rates need to be analyzed to look for differences by ethnicity or gender. Some of the leading thinking incorporates the use of rejection interviews to understand why candidates are not accepting offers. Again, using key metrics to understand the less obvious data points can yield phenomenal insight and help advance corporate racial justice within your company.

8. **Evaluate training opportunities.** Corporate training is an investment most leading companies are eager to make. However, many of the internal and external curriculum contain elements of bias that need to be eliminated. These classes can be enhanced further by editing them to contain more inclusive

language, names, images, and examples. Many companies are now reviewing external training providers to include these criteria. Companies that develop their own internal training materials and courses are editing those courses or ensuring that new courses are more inclusive. Finally, critically reviewing the needs of the diverse population beyond simple job and skills training to incorporate advanced topics and learning methods is becoming commonplace for leading companies.

9. **Analyze exit interview data.** Exit interviews provide a wealth of information. However, most exit interviews don't fully incorporate or surface issues that may drive people of color to leave. Capturing and analyzing data from exit interviews can shine a light on discriminatory practices within a company, unfair treatment, or other underlying issues. Far too often, exit interviews are captured over time and the data are analyzed after the fact and well beyond when clear action can be taken. Similar to engagement surveys, in order for exit interviews to provide value, questions must be effectively written and the responses must be analyzed promptly.

10. **Employ a racial cultural assessment.** The corporate racial cultural assessment is a method used to determine the cultural environment for diversity, equity, and inclusion within a company. This tool can be used prospectively to ensure that diverse talent has access to all the tools a company has to offer for them to succeed or retrospectively to review how and where processes or systems are breaking down preventing advancement for all.

Taking It to the Next Level

For many companies, working on the basics and getting those basics right is a significant effort and will likely take years to accomplish. But it's important to remember that advancing corporate racial justice is a journey, and we will not right four hundred years of injustices in four months. Leaders and Amplifiers need to be visionary and steadfast in their effort for continuous change. Transformational progress on corporate racial justice can be made after the basics are in motion. The first step in the next level is to take a full 360-degree view of the enterprise. This includes a comprehensive diversity, equity, and inclusion view of marketing, product development, recruiting, advancement, engagement, compensation, and representation.

Bryant advocates for corporate leaders to eliminate hurdles and create opportunities. Ann-Marie Campbell shared advice with me for leaders when they are considering employees for promotions or team assignments. Her perspective was not to look at a lesser-known individual as a risk but providing an opportunity. On reflection, it gets back to a selfish point of view: "I'm taking a risk on someone versus I'm providing an opportunity for someone." The latter is more outwardly focused and serving of their followers.

Amplifiers play a particularly important role in advancing corporate racial justice. One of the common issues surfaced when working to advance corporate racial justice is the challenge posed by our Black colleagues: "You created this problem four hundred years ago, and have perpetuated it in varying degrees since, and now you are asking us to shoulder the burden of fixing it." This challenge hits me hard. It's unfair for us to outsource the solving of corporate racial justice to our Black colleagues. This challenge was magnified during the protests and riots following the killing of George Floyd as well as the devastation and health care crisis wreaked in the Black and Hispanic communities during global COVID-19 pandemic. We made a decision to leverage our Black colleagues as advisors. We recognize that we need their input for us to improve, but we knew we needed to do the heavy lifting the change required.

Companies that have true Amplifiers of color are in a stronger position to create sustainable change. Leaders need to consciously expand their circle to include more of these Amplifiers so these activities will be done effectively. As leaders form teams to effect this change within, and given that advancement rates haven't kept up, oftentimes, leaders will need to influence their followers to rely on these Black Amplifiers to help them change perspectives, policies, and procedures.

Echo Chambers, Impact on Corporate Racial Justice

The rise of social media has given platforms for people to capture followers and disseminate their particular point of view. Information posted on these open platforms is posted and shared and reshared alike. It does not matter if the post is fact, opinion, or fiction. When posted on a social platform, too often people have a tendency to believe it. I suspect researchers are digging into the human psychology to understand why this is. For the purposes of this chapter, we will explore the followership tendencies and responsibilities that are magnified throughout the social media world.

We have seen dramatic examples of the "echo chamber of fact" as it ripples across global politics and the stock market. Political unrest fueled on social media in Hong Kong, Russia, and the US is causing significant concern. We've also seen the use of these social tools drive stock prices higher. The famous short squeeze of Game Stop and AMC Entertainment in the first quarter of 2021 are perfect examples of how social media is aligning thousands of individual interests to come together for a particular goal.

One of the key things to keep in mind is the sophistication of these technology companies and their ability to target content and advertising to their users. Depending on what sites you visit, how you interact with those sites, and other user-collected information that you volunteer, your feed is tailored to your individual user profile. The result is that we are creating digital echo chambers.

Virtually all of the social platforms are free to users. When something is free, the user is the product. For the most part, it doesn't seem that this has fazed the users of these sites, and they continue to engage and perpetuate the echo chambers. As users of social media platforms, we typically don't reflect on how our behaviors and responses are being curated in the cloud so that specific messages and targeted content will be delivered to our feed. Most of the time, it's an innocuous piece of information like an advertisement, a suggestion to watch a video of a cat eating an ice cream cone, or a prompt to see the latest design on Pinterest. But we are increasingly starting to see how we are being used in far more nefarious ways. Social media is being weaponized to create disruption or social unrest. Small bands of domestic or foreign entities can mobilize groups of people to action by taking advantage of the data being collected at the sites. In some cases, the individuals are knowingly and willingly signing up for these causes. In other cases, the users do not know that they are being played and used as pawns in others' games.

The technology behind these social media sites is only getting better. We expect technology improvements to advance at the same rate that we saw in the chip sector. The technology itself is not the issue, for it's being used for many good and useful purposes. The issue lies in the individuals processing the information being sent to them and then regurgitating that information out to their network without thought. Volume and impressions do not create truth. As long as the users fail to critically assess the information, we will not make progress.

We are seeing a large number of good people following leaders with bad intent. It is critical to study why this is occurring at such scale. In her book *Bad Leadership,* Barbara Kellerman highlights some historical leaders like Hitler who have led millions of people to do bad things. Kellerman makes a strong case that even when they know their leaders are misguided or malevolent, followers continue to follow them. She then makes the point that it's crucial that we reduce the number of bad followers.

It's hard to see in the midst of social media confusion and the corresponding echo chamber, whether a particular leader has "good" or "bad" intent. We are seeing this today in American politics. There will always be differences in positions and healthy disagreement. The vetting of those differences should lead to compromise and stability.

In 1875, Henry Drummond, the professor of natural sciences and theologian at the University of Scotland, Glasgow published a book highlighting the natural order of human interest. The lowest level is the need for self, followed by the need for family, followed by the need for society. It is in this order that followers seem to latch on to the particular carnival barker leaders propagating their positions on the social platforms. Many people live in fear that they will not achieve a certain level of material or economic prosperity, or if they have it, they fear losing it. Drummond reminds us that it's not the miser who possesses the gold, but the gold that possesses the miser. But nonetheless, fear of economic insecurity is one of the main drivers of social unrest and a ripe target for predatory leaders.

This type of leader also preys on the basic concept of peer pressure, corralling their followers like a herd of sheep to ignore their glaring character defects and self-centered motives. The followers don't even know that they are being played. It is in the best interest of society and the American way of life for there to be active and spirited debate grounded in truth. This requires that we don't just accept information as presented but that we learn how to critically think for ourselves. This is, of course, hard to do when people are feeding us information that we want to hear. Echo chambers within a company can be channeled in a positive direction by Amplifiers. However, in organizations that do not have the requisite number of Amplifiers, it can perpetuate negative culture.

Good followership demands that we critically review the information we are receiving in our own echo chambers. Amplifiers demand a comprehensive analysis of the facts, not hearsay. We all need to do a better job of fact checking and critical thinking so we can filter the information being sprayed in our direction. Being a good citizen requires us to be better followers and Amplifiers. We have a responsibility to ourselves, our families, our communities, and to future generations to make a positive impact on racial justice in our organizations now.

12 Amplifying Life

Much of our time is spent at work. For most high-need-for-achievement professionals, about one-third or more of their time each week is spent working. As a result, I always encourage people to be engaged and passionate about the work they do and the impact they make.

In the late 1850s, French painter Jean-François Millet painted *The Angelus,* a simple scene of two peasants working in a field with a church off in the distance. Millet was not a religious man. He was just capturing a childhood recollection of his grandmother who would pause to say the Angelus prayer when the church bells rang. He also wanted to capture the hard-working nature of peasant life in a simple rural scene. Henry Drummond captured the same three elements of work, spirituality, and relationships in many of his addresses in the late 1800s. It is the combination and balance of these three forces that make for a great work and life integration.

For years at Clarkston, we thought that creating differentiated results—what we call *brilliant client service*—was sufficient for long-term success. We took great pride in the quality of the work and the outcomes produced for our clients, all while standing behind the work we do. However, we are seeing an interesting convergence as new generations of workers enter the workforce. This new generation cares about company purpose: not just ours, but our clients' as well. They are energized by the work our clients do, the benefits produced, and the impact on society. Perhaps it is a spiritual awakening of the corporate variety.

We have long relied on our business relationships and the trust we develop with our fellow colleagues and our clients. We have a longer tenure with our stewards than do our competitors, because we invest in creating an environment in which their contributions are valued and respected. We have a high degree of repeat business as a direct result of the successful projects we do for our clients. We have also learned that as these executives grow in their careers, they are eager to bring us in to help them with challenges facing their new roles or at the new companies where they serve.

We see this work-life integration occurring at our clients' organizations, too, where many are investing in their people and their people's purpose. The global COVID-19 pandemic wreaked havoc across personal and professional lives around the globe. Companies are rethinking how they engage with their employees in a revised and virtual work environment. They also better appreciate their employees' desire that the organization raise the bar on societal issues, such as environmental, social, and governance improvements. The call for companies to be better stewards of the environment is taking root, and we are seeing many companies changing their long-term strategies to account for their impact on the climate. The new generation has little tolerance for corporate racial injustice or gender inequality.

Employees want to work for companies that make a positive difference in human lives; it's no longer enough to just be producing yet another version of some product. We saw the vision Indra Nooyi put forth at PepsiCo with her "better for you" and "better for the environment" strategy. We are also seeing leaders and Amplifiers encouraging their employees to live full and meaningful lives outside of the workplace. A richer and more robust life outside the workplace creates better employees inside the workplace.

One of the exercises we do in our leadership development program is to have our participants write their own retirement tributes. They then present what they would hope others would say about them including their contributions over the course of their career. Having the vision of professional accomplishments presented through a reflective lens helps to shine a light onto the path necessary to pursue today to achieve those desired accomplishments during their careers. More often than not, our participants describe a vision and ideal for how they helped people grow their careers. But in the tyranny of today and the pressure to accomplish our own tasks and activities, we often lose sight of the benefit that helping others brings to all.

Sadly, many retiring executives have a longer list of things they wish they had done than accomplishments that they actually achieved. One of the lessons I've learned was by studying the Hindu sacred treaties, specifically the "Katha Upanishad," or "The King of Death." In the story, Katha teaches a little boy, Nachiketa, not to wait until he knows he is dying to begin to live. Many people let life pass them by and don't do the things they wish they could have done until there is no time. This is as true in our professional lives as it is in our personal lives. To this end, we seek out Amplifiers who teach us how to live life to the fullest.

Some people teach us how to live, some people teach us how to die, and others teach us both. Two recent examples have touched me and taught me valuable lessons about how to be an Amplifier in life and in death.

Tim Zurliene was an executive at one of the most successful agricultural biotech and crop protection companies in the world. He was a business leader who advanced his career in various sales and marketing roles. Clarkston had the pleasure of building a strategy for him years ago. In his final months of life, he shared with me that our strategy had served as the basis for his company's acquisition of a major competitor through a transformative deal in the crop protection and agricultural biotech industry.

Tim had an amazing depth of knowledge of the industry as well as a strategic mind. He was one of the most impressive strategic thinkers I've known in business. After our strategy project, we remained close and became friends outside of work. I am grateful to have had the honor of visiting with him at his house during his final months. We would have long conversations about work and life, and life and death. He spent his life living and working to the fullest extent possible. He was a walking example of Drummond's analysis of *The Angelus*. He invested in work, his family and relationships, and his spirituality.

Even at the end, he would often work to help the team think through a strategic angle to a problem or issue they were confronting. He led up, providing candid and straightforward feedback to his bosses, and provided mentorship and development for his followers. We would often ask if it bothered him that his work still demanded his time when he knew that he wouldn't be returning. He would laugh and reiterate how grateful he was that he could still provide value to his team and that he was still sought after for his help. He was literally a lifelong learner and teacher. He did not know he was teaching us far more than work-related lessons. In fact, he was teaching us how to live a full and fulfilling life.

The other exemplary Amplifier is Bobby Menges, whose life epitomized the motto "it's not the years of life that matter, it's the life in the years." In his nineteen short years, he touched more lives and had a bigger impact on society than many do in eighty years. Bobby was diagnosed with cancer as a young child of five and dealt with the consequences of the condition daily. At nine, after a skiing accident and painful limb-lengthening surgeries, he was diagnosed with cancer for the second time. Despite this set back, Bobby embraced life and was not slowed down in his zeal to help others. He came to understand the value of service at an early age. He ran blood drives, played in his band for charity, gave speeches, ran fundraisers, and pulled other teens along with him. His ability to connect with others and know what they were going through was purely inspirational.

He had a contagious ability to connect with people, to inspire them not to focus on themselves but rather to be of service to others. This was not an easy thing to do with tweens and teens, but he got right to the essence of the issues and had the ability to influence people to fervently support a cause.

He amplified our ability to focus on our greater purpose—and do it with a ton of fun. He made a lasting impression not just for his compassion but also for his impact on society. He had to wait four years, from age ten to fourteen, until he was allowed to volunteer at his local hospital. When he was finally able to volunteer, he immediately made a difference with the patients, doctors, and administration. He was a walking example of how to live life to the fullest every day. I'm not sure if he considered the fragility and shortness of his life expectancy, but he viewed every day as a day he could make a difference or be of service to someone else. His energy and enthusiasm for life was contagious.

As he grew up, he recognized the gap that existed for adolescent and young adult (AYA) cancer patients. Pediatric and adult oncology are more common, and plenty of funding has been raised to care for these populations. Yet there exists a significant gap for teenage cancer patients, who struggle with a unique host of issues that children and older adults do not. He inspired health care administrators to create programs to support this underserved community of patients and their families. This idea strengthened as he was diagnosed with cancer for his third time as a freshman at Duke University. He was readmitted into Duke Hospital for treatment as a sophomore. I was grateful to be able to be near him and learn from his example in his final years. The AYA community is better for the contribution Bobby made and the enthusiasm he created among a whole host of followers. His legacy lives on through the I'm Not Done Yet Foundation, to which all the proceeds from this book will be donated.

****

Don't wait to be inspired. The time is now to act and to amplify your career and your life. The journey starts where your feet are. Nobody is too old or too young to change their career or their life trajectory. Build a career vision and strategy that includes your work and life goals. See to it that you are passionate about the work you are doing, because for most of us, it will consume a significant portion of our lives. Invest in your learning and growth. Build relationships with your colleagues inside and outside the company. Develop an attitude of service and mindfulness in your work to help increase its spirituality. Give freely and you will receive more. Think about what you can offer someone, the value you can add to a situation. Then and only then will you receive. In short, strive to be a True Amplifier.

Notes

Chapter 1

1. Definition from Google search: https://www.google.com/search?q=what
+are+the+dictionaries&rlz=1C1CHBF_enUS795US796&oq=what+are+
the+dictionaries&aqs=chrome..69i57j0j0i22i30l2j0i10i22i30j0i22i30l5.
12572j1j15&sourceid=chrome&ie=UTF-8 # dobs=leader.

Chapter 2

1. *Meriam-Webster,* https://www.merriam-webster.com/dictionary/charisma.
2. S&P Capital IQ, Clarkston research.
3. Jim Collins, *Good to Great* (New York: HarperCollins, 2001), 41.

Chapter 3

1. Robert Kelley, *The Power of Followership* (New York: Bantam Doubleday
Dell, 1992), 125–26.
2. Samantha Hurwitz and Marc Hurwitz, *Leadership Is Half the Story: A Fresh
Look at Followership, Leadership, and Collaboration* (Toronto: Rotman,
2015).
3. Kelley, *The Power of Followership,* 97.

Chapter 4

1. Walmart investor relations website: https://corporate.walmart.com/our-
story/leadership/executive-management/doug-mcmillon/.
2. Paul Toscano, "CNBC Portfolio's Worst American CEO's of All Time,"
April 30, 2009, www.cnbc.com/2009/04/30/Portfolios-Worst-American-
CEOs-of-all-time.html.

Chapter 5

1. Kenneth Andrews, *The Concept of Corporate Strategy* (Homewood, IL: Dow Jones-Irwin, 1971).
2. Apple investor relations website and securities filings. https://s2.q4cdn .com/470004039/files/doc_financials/2020/ar/_10-K-2020-(As-Filed) .pdf.
3. Investopedia. Foxconn iPhone City. https://www.investopedia.com/ articles/investing/090315/10-major-companies-tied-apple-supply-chain.asp.
4. Apple. https://investor.apple.com/sec-filings/default.aspx.
5. Christina Morales, "Millions of Views Later, Nathan Apodaca Keeps the Vibe Going," *New York Times,* October 7, 2020.

Chapter 6

1. Collins, *Good to Great*, 30.
2. Gary Chapman, *The Five Love Languages: The Secret to Love That Lasts* (Chicago: Northfield Publishing, 2015).
3. A. A. Milne, *Winnie-the-Pooh*. London: Methuen & Co. Ltd., 1926.
4. David Maister, Charles Green, and Robert Galford, *The Trusted Advisor* (New York: Free Press, 2004), 69.
5. Zhenhua Chen and Serena Loftus, "Multi-Method Evidence on Investors' Reactions to Managers' Self-Inclusive Language," *Accounting, Organizations and Society,* September 11, 2019, https://papers.ssrn.com/sol3/ papers.cfm?abstract_id=2950702.

Chapter 7

1. Kelley, *The Power of Followership*, 97.

Chapter 8

1. Henry Drummond, *The Greatest Thing in the World* (Philadelphia: Henry Altemus,1891), 46.
2. Nooyi, Indra. "Truths from the Top." YouTube. 2019 Women in the World Summit.

Chapter 9

1. "Business Roundtable Redefines the Purpose of a Corporation to Promote 'An Economy That Serves All Americans,'" Business Roundtable, August 19, 2019, www.businessroundtable.org/business-redefines-the-purpose-of-a-corporation-to-promote-an-economy-that-serves-all-americans.
2. Harry Robinson, "Why Do Most Transformations Fail? A Conversation with Harry Robinson," McKinsey, July 10, 2019, https://www.mckinsey.com/business-functions/transformation/our-insights/why-do-most-transformations-fail-a-conversation-with-harry-robinson.
3. S&P Capital IQ, Clarkston research.
4. Nelson Mandela and Richard Stengel, *Mandela's Way: Lessons for an Uncertain Age* (New York: Broadway Books, 2010), 113.

Chapter 10

1. John Kotter, *Leading Change* (Boston: Harvard Business School Press, 1996). This seminal publication and his numerous other works lead me to this conclusion.
2. Chobani's corporate website and articles.
3. Carol Dweck, *Mindset* (New York: Random House, 2006), 124.

Chapter 11

1. Louis Deas, "Delta Air Lines Teams Up with Operation HOPE to Support Employees Managing Their Financial Health," Operation HOPE, February 26, 2021, https://operationhope.org/announcements/delta-air-lines-teams-up-with-operation-hope-to-support-employees-managing-their-financial-health/.
2. David Thomas, "Morehouse President: It's Too Soon for Georgia to Open Up. Here's How We're Weathering the Storm," CNN, April 24, 2020, https://www.cnn.com/2020/04/24/opinions/morehouse-president-too-soon-for-georgia-to-open-thomas/index.html.
3. S&P Capital IQ, Clarkston research.

Recommended Readings

Bryant, John Hope. *Up from Nothing: The Untold Story of How We (All) Succeed.* Oakland, CA: Berrett-Koehler, 2020.

Collins, Jim. *Good to Great.* New York: HarperCollins, 2001.

Drucker, Peter. *Management: Tasks, Responsibilities, Practices.* New York: Harper & Row, 1973.

Drummond, Henry. *The Greatest Thing in the World.* London: Houghton and Stoddard, 1891.

Dweck, Carol. *Mindset: The New Psychology of Success.* New York: Random House, 2006.

Hurwitz, Samantha, and Marc Hurwitz. *Leadership Is Half the Story.* Toronto: Rotman, 2015.

Kellerman, Barbara. *Bad Leadership: What It Is, How It Happens, Why It Matters.* Boston: Harvard Business School, 2004.

Kelley, Robert. *The Power of Followership.* New York: Bantam Doubleday Dell, 1992.

Kotter, John. *A Force for Change: How Leadership Differs from Management.* New York: The Free Press, 1990.

Lewis, Michael. *Moneyball: The Art of Winning an Unfair Game.* New York: W. W. Norton, 2003.

Maister, David, Charles Green, and Robert Galford. *The Trusted Advisor.* New York: The Free Press, 2004.

Patrick, Deval. *A Reason to Believe: Lessons from an Improbable Life.* New York: Random House, 2011.

Acknowledgments

This book summarizes a journey full of observations of Amplifier behavior made by my colleagues at Clarkston, my partners and fellow stewards, my clients, trusted advisors, and my own personal interaction with many people at great companies. Without the contribution and support of these extraordinary individuals, the examples and reflection would not capture the essence of leadership, followership, and Amplifiers. In particular, I'd like to thank Irene Birbeck, Seth Brenner, John Hope Bryant, Dan Caulkins, Ann-Marie Campbell, Aaron Chio, Carrie Francis, Helena Foulkes, Paul Garrison, Tim Hassinger, Drake Jaglowski, Faith Kosobucki, Mike Leary, LaToya Lee, Ling Lin, Liz Menges, Brandon Miller, Sara Morris, Neil Nelson, former governor Deval Patrick, David Patterson, Zach Schisgal, Jim Stefan, Michelle Tartalio, Jim Theis, and Sebastian Valencia. Their encouragement and contribution to the work is greatly appreciated.

About the Author

Tom Finegan is a serial entrepreneur, trusted advisor, investor and leadership expert. Tom is the founder and CEO of Clarkston Consulting and has over 30 years of experience in consulting working with some of the world's most respected companies, with expertise in business strategy, leadership, and driving business growth. As co-founder, chairman, and chief executive officer of Clarkston Consulting, Tom has defined and executed the firm's strategy since the company's origination in 1991.

Tom believes consulting firms must genuinely care about driving measurable business results for clients and creating a rewarding and stimulating environment for professionals to thrive in the crowded consulting marketplace. Under Tom's leadership, this strategy has been successful, and Clarkston has achieved an industry-leading net promoter score of 89% and a client satisfaction rating of 97% over the last twenty years.

Tom has applied his experience and leadership philosophy in his forthcoming book, *Amplifiers*. In his book, Tom explores how leaders can develop and nurture true Amplifiers – individuals who combine both leadership and followership to influence up, lead others, and execute the mission of the business.

Twice named a finalist in Ernst & Young's Entrepreneur of the Year, a 40 under 40 Leader, three-time Inc500 recipient, and other industry awards, Tom is recognized in the industry as an entrepreneurial strategist able to bring new innovative ideas to large and emerging companies alike. As a proven leader and a recognized expert in transformational strategy development, Tom still serves as an adviser and advocate for global life sciences and consumer products companies.

Tom is active in the community, co-managing member of Clarkston Merchant Partners and serves on the boards of FoodLogiQ, Momentum, and CelerPurus.

Index

NOTE: Page references in *italics* refer to figures.